My Favorite
Bible

Presented To

From

On

My Favorite
Bible

The Best-Loved Stories of the Bible

Rondi DeBoer and Christine Tangvald

Illustrated by Ariel Pang

Revell

a division of Baker Publishing Group
Grand Rapids, Michigan

Text © 2011 by Rondi DeBoer and Christine Tangvald
Illustrations © 2011 by Ariel Pang

Published by Revell
a division of Baker Publishing Group
P.O. Box 6287, Grand Rapids, MI 49516-6287
www.revellbooks.com

ISBN 978-0-8007-1956-2

Library of Congress Cataloging-in-Publication Data
DeBoer, Rondi.
    My favorite Bible : the best-loved stories of the Bible / Rondi DeBoer and Christine Tangvald ; illustrated by Ariel Pang.
        p.   cm.
    ISBN 978-0-8007-1956-2 (cloth)
    1. Bible stories, English. I. Tangvald, Christine Harder, 1941– II. Pang, Ariel.
III. Title.
BS551.3.D432 2011
220.9′505—dc22   2011004046

Scripture quotations are from God's Word®. © 1995 God's Word to the Nations. Used by permission of Baker Publishing Group.

Published in association with the literary agency of Alive Communications, Inc., 7680 Goddard Street, Suite 200, Colorado Springs, CO 80920. www.alivecommunications.com.

Interior Design by Michael J. Williams

13   14   15   16   17   18   19   8   7   6   5   4   3   2

Rondi

To my daughters
Rachael, Emma, Belle, and Jada
May the Lord illuminate your hearts
to the truth of the glorious gospel of Jesus.
And may you, by grace through faith, find joy forever with Him!
I love you, my sweet girls.

To Brian
Thank you for speaking the gospel into my life.
To have been blessed with a life by your side
is truly, deeply beyond words.
I love you.

To my mother
Every word you have ever written for the glory of God . . . is a classic.
Writing with you is one of the great joys of my life.
Thank you, Mama. I love you.

Christine

To Rondi Lucille DeBoer
My beautiful daughter,
My glorious fun-filled friend,
My heart-to-heart mentor,
My dedicated coauthor.
Thank you for pouring every ounce of your being into the writing of this book.
And as we prayed together before the first word was set to paper,
may God be pleased.
May every word of every story reflect His Glory to all who read it.

I love you, Rondi. You are AWESOME!

CONTENTS

New Testament

9

WELCOME, MY FRIEND . . .

I'm so excited to read these Bible stories with you!

Stories of bravery.
Stories of adventure.
Stories of warriors, children, and miracles.

But the Bible is not just a book of good stories.
No!
It is a true book
inspired by God
that shows us:
who God is
what He has done
and how we should respond to Him.

You see, the Bible is a very special book about
an amazing God . . .
who makes a big promise

to send a loving Savior, Jesus,
so that we may live joyfully with God forever!

Living joyfully with God sounds good, doesn't it?
Oh, it is!

This promise of God is the focus
of the whole Bible.
Every story reflects the Promised One.
Every event prepares the way for His coming.
Every page proclaims the truth that

Jesus

is our one and only Savior.

So be excited with me!
Turn the page and let's get started.

God's promise is big.
God's promise is for you.
Read it. Believe it. Rejoice in it.

Note to Adults

A **Family Talk** page with a *Faith Foundation* and *Key Verse* ends each story. Read this section out loud with your children and let the discussion questions become a springboard into teaching, wonder, and free conversation about daily and spiritual matters. Not every question must be answered. Just enjoy the open communication about the most important topics in life. Treasure this time.

The **Family Fun** section is a great place to live and laugh together. Do as many activities as you can—and even make up a few of your own! Don't be afraid to be silly. Your children will remember your laughter for years to come.

The final option on each of these ideas is a drawing suggestion. You may want to save these pieces of artwork in a three-ring **Bible Story Binder.** As you progress through the Bible, kids will love creating their own book of Bible stories.

Seek-and-Find Fun. There are seventy-seven butterflies for children to find in the illustrations throughout the book. Point out the first, and ask them to look for the rest. It's another great way to engage children in the visual part of each story.

Pray with Your Children. Pray about the story. Pray about the *Faith Foundation.* Pray about their day and their worries and their joys. The moments you spend with them are some of the most important moments of your day—and some of the most precious in your life. How awesome and wonderful that you are spending time together loving and learning about the wonderful gift of eternal life with God through faith in Jesus.

OLD TESTAMENT

GOD CREATES

Creation of the World—Genesis 1:1–25

In the beginning, there was God.

God the Father.

God the Son.

God the Holy Spirit.

And He was happy!

Then God decided to do something wonderful.
God decided to do something simply amazing.
He decided to create a world that would bring Him
perfect glory.

And so . . . He spoke.

"Let there

be!"

And suddenly, there was!

"Light!"

Flash!
Bright light shone into the darkness,
radiating God's power
for the world He was about to create.

"Heavens!"

Brilliant blue skies pulled away upward
from the rushing waters below.
Sweet, fresh air flew fast over the earth.

"Land!"

Dry dirt appeared—
from the tops of soaring mountain peaks
all the way down to deep cracks and crevasses
in low-lying canyons.

"Plants!"

Apples, oranges, bananas, and pears
dripped with sweetness
on branches stretched
up, up, up—declaring *God is good.*
Berry bushes, wildflowers, and desert grasses
burst into bloom and gave the earth unending color.

"Stars!"

God's voice rumbled and rolled,
loud and strong,
to the outer edges of the universe.
Bright stars lit up for the first time
as His Word was spoken.

The great sun He made to rule the day
and the gentle moon to govern the night,
as if to say at all times
God is king.

"Animals!"

Tiny striped fish and whooshing whales
danced together with joy in the seas.

Rainbow-feathered birds
swooped and soared
over the earth
in praise to God, their Creator.

"More animals!"

Elephants trumpet.

Cows moo.

Kittens meow.

Owls *Whoo? Whoo? Whoo?*

Who has made us? They screeched and roared.

God did! God did!

Praise—that's what animal voices are for.

Every animal that has ever been,

joined in jubilee,

giving glory to the God of all,

who made them each so wonderfully.

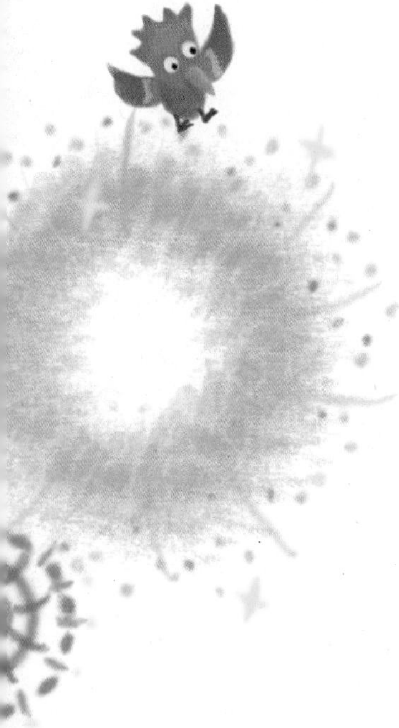

God looked down
on the light
and the dark
and the wind
and the waves
and the mountains
and the valleys
and the trees
and the fruit
and the sun
and the stars
and the feathers
and the fur

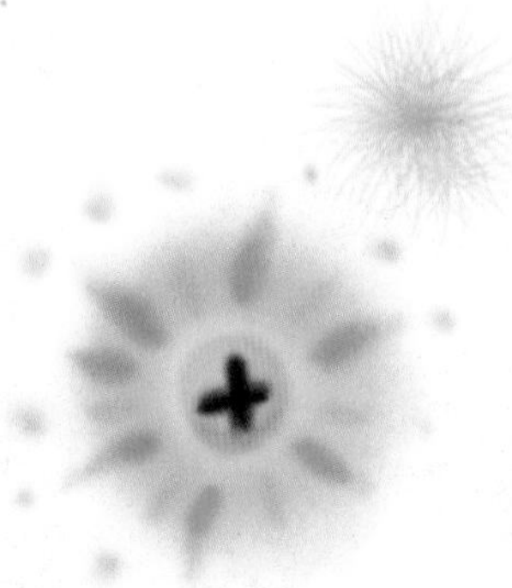

and declared with authority for all to hear

"It is good!"

FAMILY TALK

Faith Foundation:

God Created All Things for His Glory

 Key Verse

In the beginning God created heaven and earth.

Genesis 1:1

Everything in creation shows us a little bit about the amazing God who made it. His creation reveals His glory. Yes, all that God has created continually shows us the awesome nature of God.

A turtle can show us God is patient.
Pure white snow can show us God is holy.
Lightning can show us God is powerful.
Sweet fruit can show us God is good.

What is your favorite creation of God?
Why do you like it so much?
What is something you see about God in your favorite
   creation?

FAMILY FUN

A Nature Walk Collage

Option #1
Grab a basket or bag and go for a nature walk as a family. Collect pieces of God's beautiful creation as you go (leaves, rocks, flowers, etc.). When you get home, create a fantastic collage of God's creation by gluing your treasures on a giant poster board or paper plate. Share your glimpses of God's glory with each other.

Option #2
Study a rock or shell collection—or a beautiful flower. Be amazed at all the detailed creations of God.

Option #3
Draw a magnificent picture of your favorite thing from creation. (Parents: you may want to save the drawings in a three-ring binder—a Bible Story Binder—as you progress through *My Favorite Bible*. Kids love to make their own books and have something to show others!)

GOD CREATES AGAIN

Creation of Adam and Eve—Genesis 1:26–2:23

God was not finished quite yet.
He had one more very special creation left to do.
Do you know what God created last of all?

People!

But God made people differently
than He made the light.
He made them differently than He made the stars.
He made them differently
than He made the plants that grow
and the animals that swim, and creep, and fly.

God didn't say a word.

God scooped up dust of the earth
into His awesome hands
and formed man in His own image.

He rolled man's legs.
He fashioned man's hair.
He sculpted each bone and muscle
with careful, loving strokes.

And when He was done . . .

God smiled.

Whoooooooooo

With the wild wind of His great breath
God blew into man's nose
and gave him
life.

oosh!

This man was named
Adam.

From one of Adam's ribs
God gently and beautifully formed a woman
in His own image.

Her name was
Eve.

Adam and Eve loved each other very much.
Adam and Eve loved God very much.

And God, their Creator,
loved both Adam and Eve

exceedingly
abundantly
and
forever.

God looked down on His last addition
to creation and said,

"Behold, it is *very* good!"

FAMILY TALK

Faith Foundation:

God Created All People in His Own Image

So God created humans in his image.
In the image of God he created them.
He created them male and female.
Genesis 1:27

Adam and Eve were created in God's image. But God didn't stop there. Oh, no! God created each and every person that has ever lived in the whole world in His very own image. Even you and me. Isn't that amazing? That means some very wonderful and special qualities about you are somehow like the God who created you.

You have emotions to love God and others.

You have the power to choose right over wrong.

You have a soul that can know God and live forever in heaven someday.

And the longer you live and love God, the more like Him you will become!

Are you glad God made men and women, boys and girls . . . like you?

How does being made in God's image make you want to act?

Will becoming more like God make you happier? Why?

# FAMILY FUN

Encouragement Ring

Option #1 God made everyone special. Let's create an encouragement ring. Sit in a circle. Take turns sitting in the middle. Now, think carefully about the person in the middle. Have everyone tell two special things they really like about the person in the center. Whose turn is next?

Option #2 Sing the song, "Head, Shoulders, Knees and Toes." Touch each body part with both hands as you say it!

Head and shoulders, knees and toes, knees and toes
Head and shoulders, knees and toes, knees and toes
Eyes and ears and mouth and nose
Head and shoulders, knees and toes, knees and toes

Guess what? God made ALL of those!

Option #3 Draw a beautiful picture of yourself showing how special God created you. Don't forget to include your big smile! Add this picture to your Bible Story Binder.

THE PROMISE

The Fall—Genesis 3

Adam and Eve held hands
and joyfully walked with God
in the Garden of Eden.
It was a sweet and perfect
friendship and fellowship
between God and His creation.

Adam was happy.

Eve was happy.

And God was happy.

In God's garden grew many trees
with delicious fruit for Adam and Eve.

Crunchy apples and juicy oranges.
Precious pears and ruby-red cherries.
Green grapes, prickly pineapples,
and bunches upon bunches of bananas
were all available for Adam and Eve
to eat anytime.

But . . .

In the very center
of the garden God placed
a very special tree.
A lovely tree
with juicy fruit
swaying softly
in the breeze.

***It was the Tree of the
Knowledge of Good and Evil.***

God, in His wisdom, told Adam and Eve,
"You can eat from any other tree in the garden, but

do not eat from this tree!"

To eat from this tree would bring death.
So, Adam and Eve obeyed God . . . for a while.

Now, in the garden
was a snake.
He was a slippery, shifty,
and sneaky serpent.

He did not want Adam and Eve to obey God.
That snake wanted them to obey him.
He did not want Adam and Eve to give glory to God.
That snake wanted God's glory for himself.

And so, that selfish snake tempted Adam and Eve
to eat the forbidden fruit by telling
a terrible lie.

"This tree won't bring death," he hissed . . .
"It will make you wise.
This fruit will make you like God!"

We can be like God? wondered Adam.
We can be like God? wondered Eve.
To be like God sounded good to Adam and Eve.

When they looked at the beautiful,
sweet, delicious fruit,
Adam and Eve thought *they* should decide
what is right
what is best
what is true
for themselves.

They decided to disobey God.
And they picked the forbidden fruit.
And they ate the sweetness.
And then . . .
they hid.

Oh, yes! They tried to hide from God!
As soon as they ate that fruit,
they knew it was wrong . . .
so wrong to disobey God!

When we disobey God, it is called sin.
Sin separates us from God.
And Adam and Eve's hearts grew heavy
with their great sin against God.

Soon . . . God came,
filled with sorrow
that Adam and Eve had destroyed
their sweet and perfect
friendship and fellowship with Him.

Sin must be punished.

And so Adam and Eve must leave
the perfect garden
God had made.

Now life would be hard for Adam and Eve.
Now their children would sin.
And now their bodies would grow old and die.

And most importantly,
no one would be able to live joyfully
with God like before,
because sin had entered the hearts of people.
And God, in His holiness, cannot be close to sin.

Oh! What a sad and sorrowful day.
But . . .

This is not the end of the story.

No. This is just the beginning!

Because you see, God made His people a promise.
The most important promise ever made.

He promised something amazing.
He promised something wonderful.
He promised something unbelievably kind
and merciful and loving.

God promised that
He would not leave us in our sin . . .
separated from Himself.

He would send the Promised One.

A Savior
who would take away our sin,
so we can all someday live joyfully with God forever!

FAMILY TALK

 Faith Foundation:

God Promises a Savior from Sin

I find joy in your promise
like someone who finds a priceless treasure.
Psalm 119:162

God made a promise—a wonderful promise! He made a promise that is a treasure for you and me. This promise was a declaration by God Himself to do something wonderful for us: to send us the Promised One, a Savior, who will take away all our sin.

That is a big promise, isn't it? But God can do anything. He is good, strong, and merciful enough to keep His promise. Oh, yes! Our God is forever faithful. He always keeps His promises!

What promise has someone made to you?

Why will God keep His promise to us?

How happy does it make you to know that God will save us from sin? Show me with your arms outstretched.

FAMILY FUN

The Promised One Poster

Make a beautiful promise poster by writing the words:

The Promised One

in large, open letters. Fill each letter with decorations such as jewels, flowers, swirls, stars, stickers, and colorful squiggly lines to represent the hope we have in God's promise. God is faithful—He has sent us the Promised One, our Savior. Hang your poster where you can see it often.

Draw a picture of the Tree of the Knowledge of Good and Evil with delicious, juicy fruit. Maybe you'll want to add the sneaky, slithery snake! Add this picture to your Bible Story Binder.

AWESOME ARK

The Flood—Genesis 6:1–9:17

Outside the Garden of Eden,
Adam and Eve had children.
Those children grew up, got married,
and had more children.

And those children had children.
And those children had children.
And those children had children.

Until the whole wide world
was covered with people!
Lots and lots of people.
But, sadly, these people did not love and obey God.

Only one man did.
Only one man loved and obeyed God
and had a wonderful relationship with Him.
And this man's name was

Noah.

Noah loved God.
And God loved Noah.

One day, God whispered,
"I'm sending a rain."

Noah hushed to hear.

God warned,
"I'm sending a flood."

Noah leaned in to listen.

*"I'm sending a judgment
to destroy the earth!"*

Then, God commanded,
"Noah, make an ark!"

Noah obeyed, and built a big, huge boat
out of gopher wood.
Then . . . all of God's animals entered in
seven by seven and two by two
and that awesome ark became a floating zoo
with zebras, hippos, and cockatoos.
And Noah listened to the roaring
and the squeaking.
The flapping! The stomping! The tromping!
The bleating and the tweeting
and the hissing and the trumpeting,
and stood amazed!

Amazed as he gazed upon God's plan of salvation.
God knew exactly how He would save His creation.
He provided the one and only way . . .

The Ark.

Drip. Drip.
Drop. Drop.
Drip. Drop.

Whooooosh!

The rain came down.
It sprinkled, it splashed,
it rushed and it gushed,
as it poured out of the dark cloudy sky!

Have you ever seen a thunderstorm?
Well, this was the biggest storm there ever was!

Crash! Flash! The bright lightning
sliced the sky with electric bolts.

Noah and his family
rushed to climb into the ark, and then . . .

Slam!

God closed the door.

For forty days and forty nights
the rains poured down from the blackened sky
until . . .
all the flowers sunk underwater,
all the houses sunk underwater,
all the treetops sunk underwater,
and even the mighty mountains themselves
seemed to be

swallowed up by the sea.

The whole earth was completely covered
in waves upon waves of water.

Noah prayed,
the animals swayed,
floating safely in God's ark.

But God never forgot Noah
and His plan of salvation.

Whooooooooooh!

God sent a great wind to blow over the earth.

Whooooooooooh!

The waters dried up and the ark came to rest
on Mount Ararat.

Slowly, slowly, the turtles peeked
and poked their heads out.
Slowly, slowly, the pigs waddled across the floor
and out the door.
Then quickly, wildly, and excitedly
all the animals scrambled out of the ark!

Birds flew in the new blue skies.
Bees buzzed in the sweet fresh air.
And all of the animals basked
in God's glorious warm sunlight.

Oh! The wonderful plan of God!
Noah built an altar to the Lord
and thanked God for
His one way of salvation,
the ark.
Then God painted a rainbow
of many colors across the sky
as a sign of His promise
to never destroy the earth by flood again.

So when you look up
and see a beautiful rainbow after a storm,
please remember:

God always keeps His promises!

FAMILY TALK

Faith Foundation:

God Provided the Only Way to Be Saved

 Key Verse

I (God) will put my rainbow in the clouds to be a sign of my promise to the earth.

Genesis 9:13

Before the rain came pouring down, God told Noah to build an awesome ark that would save him and his family from the rising waters.

The Promised One is like that ark. He is the only way to be saved from the flood of our sin. Like the one door of the ark that Noah and the animals went through to be saved, the Promised One is our one door, the only way we can enter into a joyful life with God forever.

God set a rainbow in the clouds and promised Noah that He would never destroy the earth by flood again. He kept His promise. God also said He would send the Promised One to save us from sin, and He kept that promise too . . . just keep reading!

What is your favorite part of this Bible story?
How would you feel if you were Noah on the ark?
Have you ever seen a rainbow?

FAMILY FUN

Which Animal Am I?

Option #1

Let's pretend to be an animal going onto Noah's huge ark. Which animal will you choose to be? Shhh . . . don't tell anyone. It's a secret. Everyone will have to guess!

Will you be a roaring lion? A soaring eagle? Will you be a trumpeting elephant? An itsy bitsy bug? You can slide and glide, leap and jump, stomp or creep, or hop, hop, hop.

Everyone take a turn. One at a time, pretend to be your secret animal. Everyone must guess which animal you are until they get it right. Do it again and again!

Option #2

Draw an awesome picture of Noah's ark on dry land, with the animals running out. Don't forget the rainbow! Add this picture to your Bible Story Binder.

FATHER OF FAITH

Abraham—Genesis 15:1–7

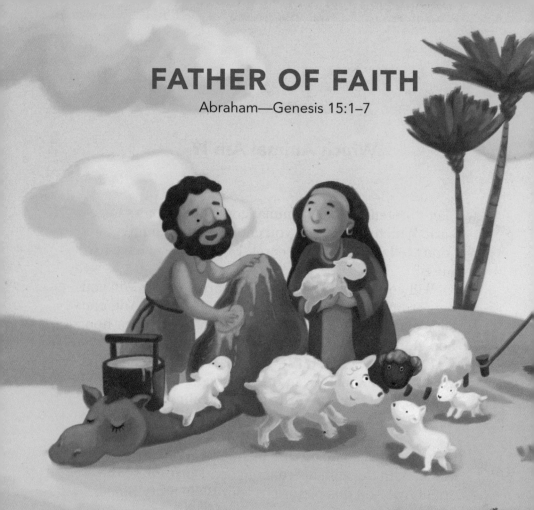

There once was a man named Abram.
Abram means

"Good Father."

Abram wanted to be a good father,
but he had a problem.
He didn't have any children!
Not one boy.
Not one girl.
No children at all in his family!

When Abram was very old,
99 years old,
probably older than your grandmother
or even your great-grandmother,
God appeared to him.

"I am God Almighty.

I promise to give you a son.
From now on
your name will be . . .

Abraham!"

Because Abraham means
"Father of Many."

Father of many? Abraham wondered.
How big will my family be?

"Look at the heavens,"
God said.

"Can you count
the sparkling stars
in the dark night sky?"

Abraham looked up, up, up.
His eyes squinted as he searched the deep darkness.
Tiny dots of twinkling light met his gaze.

Tens.
Hundreds.
Thousands.
Millions of stars shone above him.

"That is how big your family will be!
As many as the stars in the sky!"
Countless boys.
Countless girls.
All in one family.

How can my family be so big? thought Abraham.
He didn't know.
But Abraham believed God.

He believed God's promise . . .
by faith.

And did you know that God kept His promise?
He did.
Abraham and his wife, Sarah, had a baby boy,
a son, named Isaac.

And Isaac had a son named Jacob.

And through Jacob came
many, many, many, many children.

But God kept His promise to Abraham
in a bigger way as well.

You see, Abraham put his faith in God
and joined God's family.

And the Bible says that
anyone who puts all their faith
in God and His Promised One
becomes a part of God's family too.

It's true!
Even me! Even you!

**We can be in God's family
by faith in the Promised One.**

By faith alone.

When Abraham looked into the sky
that amazing night
and tried to count the multitude of stars,
**he saw one star for each person
in the family of God.**

Just think . . .
One star had been lit for Adam.
One star had been lit for Eve.
Three stars had been lit
for Abraham, Joseph, and Moses.
Millions of stars for millions of people
across the world
and throughout the ages.

One star had even been lit for me.

**And one special star
that twinkled at Abraham
may have been lit
for you!**

FAMILY TALK

Faith Foundation:

We Are Part of God's Family by Faith

Key Verse

He (God) took Abram outside and said, "Now look up at the sky and count the stars, if you are able to count them." He also said to him, "That's how many descendants you will have!" Then Abram believed the LORD, and the LORD regarded that faith to be his approval of Abram."

Genesis 15:5–6

Did you know that God has a HUGE family? He does. With too many people to name! You were born or adopted into your family, but to be in God's family you must enter by faith. Not just faith in God, or faith in His Word, but by faith in His Promised One and His plan of saving us from our sin.

By faith in the Promised One, we are forgiven.

By faith in the Promised One, we are brought near to God.

And by faith in the Promised One, we become part of God's family.

Oh, yes, by faith, God is our Father forever and ever!

Who is in your family? Tell me their names.

What is the most fun part of being in a family?

What do you think would be the best thing about being in the family of God?

FAMILY FUN

Twinkle, Twinkle, Special Star!

Option #1
Draw and cut out a *big* star for each person in your family. You can cover your star with tin foil, paint it, decorate it, or just use yellow paper. In big letters, write your name on both sides of your very own star. Tape a piece of string to the top of each star. Hang all the stars together in a window or from the ceiling, or tape them to a mirror. Don't they look wonderful?

Option #2
Go outside and look up at God's twinkling sky. How many stars do you see? Can you find the Big Dipper? Ask someone to tell you about God's amazing night sky.

Option #3
Draw a beautiful picture of the starry sky Abraham saw that night. Which star is for me? Which star is for you? Can you count the stars? Add this picture to your Bible Story Binder.

DREAMER

Joseph—Genesis 37; 39–50

There was a man named Jacob.
And Jacob had many sons,
including a boy named
Joseph.

Jacob and his family were God's people.
Now Joseph was a
daring dreamer.

He dreamed of being a mighty ruler.
He dreamed of his brothers bowing down to him.
He dreamed of doing great things
for God and His people.
But Joseph's dreams made his brothers jealous.
Very jealous.
And very, very angry.

Joseph's brothers discussed
and devised a dangerous plan.

"We are tired of the dreamer," they whispered.
"We are tired of all the attention he gets."

So they snatched him away,
sold him away,
and sent him off . . . far, far away
to be a slave in the land of Egypt.

But, through it all, Joseph trusted God.
And God had a
good plan
for Joseph's life.

Joseph worked hard as a slave in Egypt.
He was mistreated and sent to jail
for something he did not do.

From the dark, damp prison cell Joseph thought,
This is not the dream I had.

Oh, what should Joseph do?
Should he give up on God?
No!
Through it all, Joseph still trusted God.
And God had a
good plan
for Joseph's life.

One day, God took Joseph out of that prison cell
and sent him to Pharaoh's great palace.
"I hear you are a dreamer!"
said Pharaoh.
"Joseph, can you tell me
the meaning of my dreams?"
As Pharaoh told about his strange dreams,
God revealed the meaning to Joseph.
"In seven years, there will be no food
for anyone!" Joseph said.
A famine is coming!
Pharaoh was amazed!
Pharaoh was astounded!

And so, Pharaoh made Joseph
a mighty ruler over all of Egypt.
Joseph wisely collected food
into many storehouses
to save Egypt from the famine.
"This is just like my dreams!"
exclaimed Joseph.

And then, the great and terrible famine
swept over the sun-scorched land.
No grain could grow.
No animals could graze.
No one could find food for their families . . .
anywhere!

Far away, Joseph's father, Jacob, was hungry.
Joseph's brothers were hungry.
Their wives,
their children,
and their grandchildren
were all so very hungry!

But, through it all, Joseph trusted God.
And God had a
good plan
for Joseph's life.

Now, Joseph's brothers heard of the
wise and wonderful ruler
who helped save the land of Egypt
from the famine.

*Maybe we can buy some grain
for our families there*, they thought.

And so, the brothers left for Egypt.

But as they traveled and trudged
across the barren sandy land,
their hearts grew heavy inside of them.
They remembered how they once
sold their brother
Joseph
into slavery.

They were sad,
and they were sorry.

"May we buy some grain?"
The brothers bowed down low
before the mighty Egyptian ruler.
Joseph was surprised!
Joseph was shocked!

Here were his very own brothers,
the ones who had sold him,
bowing low before him,
just like in his dreams.

Joseph's heart didn't fill with anger.
It didn't fill with hatred.

Through it all, Joseph had trusted God.
And God, in His good plan, filled Joseph's heart with
forgiveness.

When the time was right, Joseph proclaimed,
"I am your brother Joseph.
I forgive you.
What you meant for bad, God has meant for good!"

Joseph brought all of God's people to Egypt.
His father, Jacob.
His brothers.
Their wives.
Their children.
And their grandchildren.

Joseph gave them
good land and plenty of food.

Joseph's dreams came true.

Yes, through it all, he trusted God.
And God fulfilled
His good plan
for Joseph's life.

FAMILY TALK

Faith Foundation:

God Has a Good Plan

Key Verse

Even though you planned evil against me (Joseph), God planned good to come out of it.

Genesis 50:20

Everyone has dreams. Some people dream of adventure and travel. Others dream of becoming a sports star or a ballerina. Still others dream of having a family, or starting a business, or becoming a missionary. Yes, we all have dreams and plans for our lives that match the talents and desires that God created us to have. God loves to watch us dream.

But things may not always go as we planned. Sometimes we get what we want, but sometimes we don't. Sometimes our life can be fun and exciting, but sometimes it can be hard and difficult, like Joseph's.

But just like Joseph, we can trust God through it all.

His plans are good. Yes, we can trust the God who loves us, because He always has a good plan for our lives.

Like Joseph forgave his brothers, God's good plan for the Promised One is to forgive all who believe in Him!

What dreams do you have?

Do you trust God with your life? Why?

FAMILY FUN

Joseph's Sharing and Caring Jar

Option #1
Is anyone hungry where you live? During the great famine, Joseph cared . . . and shared all the food he had saved in his storehouses with hungry people everywhere.

Let's make a Caring Jar. Have fun decorating a medium size jar or box with pens, paint, sparkle glue, ribbon, or stickers. Set the jar out for everyone to drop in spare change. Let the children earn coins to give. Clink! Clunk!

When the jar is full, count the money together. Make a plan together. Make a shopping list together. Buy the food and deliver it, *together*, to help serve a family in need or a local shelter. Practice making a difference in someone's life . . . just like Joseph did. How else can you care and share with others where you live?

Option #2
Draw a picture of Joseph in Egypt, or a picture of yourself doing what you dream of doing when you grow up. Add this picture to your Bible Story Binder.

SAVED FROM SLAVERY

Moses—Exodus 3–14

Many years passed.

God's people in Egypt grew in number
and became strong.
So strong, that the new Pharaoh was terrified
they might try to take over all of Egypt!

So the Egyptians forced
all of God's people to become slaves.

God's people, full of sorrow,
cried out for deliverance.

"See us!
Shield us!
Save us, O God!"

And God heard their cries
and remembered His promises
and spoke to a man named
Moses.

"Moses! Moses!"

A powerful voice rumbled and roared and rolled
out of a blazing, burning bush.

"I am God,
and I am sending you to Pharaoh.
I will set my people free."

"Me, God?" Moses asked.
Moses couldn't believe his ears.
He didn't think he could do it.

And he was right.
Moses couldn't do it.
But God could.

Only God could fight this battle.
Only God could save His people.
**Only God could set
His people free!**

Moses bravely spoke to Pharaoh,
"God says,
'Let my people go free!'"

But Pharaoh hardened his heart against God
like a cold rock.

"I do not know this God,"
he said.
"I will not let His people go free."

There was nothing Moses could do.

But God could do anything!
Only God could save His people.
Only God could set His people free.

So God sent many
horrible plagues on Egypt to show
His glory.

All the water turned to blood.
Frogs, gnats, and flies
swarmed people and their homes.
Livestock died.
Still Pharaoh hardened his heart against God.

Boils. Hail. Locusts. Darkness.

Still Pharaoh hardened
his heart against God.

Until the last plague.
That great and terrible plague!
Thankfully, God provided a way
for His people to be safe:
the Passover lamb.

The families that obeyed God
and sacrificed this lamb were saved.
But the firstborn son of every other family died.

Pharaoh's heart began to change.
He broke. He spoke.

"Yes. God's people may go."

Have you ever been so happy you wanted to sing?
Well, that's how happy God's people were.
God's people sang praises to God
as they packed up
and hurried out of Egypt toward a
new life
of freedom.

Moses quickly led God's people to the Red Sea.
Suddenly, they heard the sound
of thundering horses' hooves
pounding the ground.
Pharaoh's army was coming!

Pharaoh had hardened his heart
against God one last time.
He came to destroy God's people.

"Help us! Save us!" cried God's people.
Again, Moses could do nothing.

But God could.

Yes, only God could save His people.
Only God could set His people free.

"The Lord is fighting for you!"
shouted Moses,
"so be still!"

Moses stretched his hand over the sea.

Whoooooo! Whooooooo!

Whooooosh!

A great shaking wind
blew upon the face of the sea.
Water washed upward and outward
until there was a path of dry land.
God led His people safely to the other side.

Then, without warning, the water crashed down
on the Egyptians following behind.

God had saved His people!
God had set His people free!

FAMILY TALK

Faith Foundation:

Only God Can Set His People Free

Key Verse

I am the LORD. I will bring you out from under the oppression of the Egyptians, and I will free you from slavery. I will rescue you with my powerful arm and with mighty acts of judgment. Then I will make you my people, and I will be your God.

Exodus 6:6–7

It is still God who sets His people free from slavery today.

Our sin against God is like having chains on our hands and feet, keeping us powerless to do what is right and good. Our hearts cry out for freedom. Only God's Promised One can save us from the slavery of sin. He breaks our chains and sets us free! Free to do what is right. What is good. What is pleasing to God.

Yes, it was true for Moses and God's people in Egypt.

It is still true for us today.

Only God can save His people.

Only God can set His people free!

What is your favorite part of the story of Moses? Why?

Imagine walking through the Red Sea. What would you see? Hear? Say?

FAMILY FUN

The Chase . . . the Race . . . to the Red Sea

Make a line of cardboard boxes to represent the shore of the Red Sea. Choose one person to be the leader, Moses. All others are the children of God. Act out the story. Pretend the Egyptians are chasing you! Moses raises his staff and stretches his arms high over the Red Sea.

Whoosh! Swoosh!
Make a hole in the line of boxes to create a safe path "through the Red Sea" for all the children of God to cross into safety. "It's a miracle! God has saved us. He has set His people free."

Trade parts and repeat. Have fun!

Frog jump! Crouch down and jump like the frogs God sent in the terrible plague on Egypt. How high can you jump? How far? Have a frog relay.

Draw an exciting picture of Moses crossing the Red Sea. Add this picture to your Bible Story Binder.

THE GOOD LAW

The Ten Commandments—Exodus 20:1–17

God wanted to give His people
written rules to help them
know right from wrong.

His rules used to be written
on every person's heart,
but sin darkened people's hearts,
and sadly they disobeyed God.

Moses climbed up Mt. Sinai and
God Himself wrote these
Ten Commandments
on two tablets made of stone
for His people to learn and obey.

Wow! Imagine!
Ten laws for life
written by
the very finger of God!

God said:

1. Worship only Me. I am the one and only true God. All glory is mine.

2. Do not make any idols or images to worship. Worship Me, instead, in spirit and in truth.

3. Use My name only in good and pure ways. Speak the truth about who I am. Do not use My name in a bad way.

4. Rest on the seventh day of the week. It is a holy day set apart for worshiping Me.

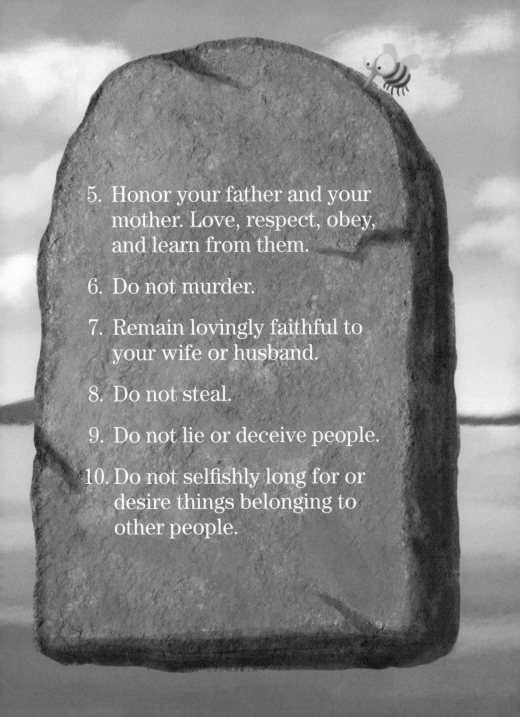

5. Honor your father and your mother. Love, respect, obey, and learn from them.

6. Do not murder.

7. Remain lovingly faithful to your wife or husband.

8. Do not steal.

9. Do not lie or deceive people.

10. Do not selfishly long for or desire things belonging to other people.

FAMILY TALK

Faith Foundation:

God's Law Is Good

 Key Verse

Indeed, your written instructions make me happy.
They are my best friends.

Psalm 119:24

God knows what is best, so He gave His written rules to help us. These rules help us know right from wrong. They help us know how to please God. They help us have a happier life. Yes, God's laws are good.

But His rules help us in another way: they help us see that we will never be able to obey God completely. They show us where we have sinned and that we desperately need a Savior. The Ten Commandments show us our need for God's saving grace and make us look to the Promised One in hope and faith.

None of us can be good enough on our own.

We need the Promised One to take away our sin!

And He does—just keep reading to find out how.

What rules do you have in your house?

Why are they good?

FAMILY FUN

My Family's Top Ten

 Draw a big tablet of stone. As a family, create for yourselves the top ten good rules for your home. Which rules will make the family the happiest? The safest? The most fun?

 The Ten Commandments are an important part of God's Holy Word—the Bible. Let's rejoice by singing together. Try jumping rope or marching while singing this song.

> The B—I—B—L—E.
> Yes, that's the book for me.
> I stand alone on the Word of God.
> The B—I—B—L—E.

 Draw a picture of Moses carrying the two big tablets of stone.

> Add this picture to your binder.

A FIGHT OF FAITH

David and Goliath—1 Samuel 17

Young David loved his sheep.
He was a kind and good shepherd.

David loved to **help** them,
care for them,
guide them,
and keep them **safe**.

Whenever a lion or bear,
licking its lips,
would sneak up and creep up to steal a snack,
David would leap out,
whirling and twirling his mighty sling
to save his precious lambs.

One day, David rushed to the battlefield
to find his brothers.
God's people were at war!

A giant warrior named
Goliath

wore a shining bronze helmet on his head,
and a long spear slung between his shoulders.

He stood high before the people of God
and mocked them as he laughed,
"Ha! Ha! Ha!
The armies of God are powerless against me!"

He lifted his voice in a challenge,
"Who will dare to fight me?"

"I will fight Goliath!" David shouted.
The soldiers **gasped**.

"I can beat lions.
I can beat bears.
And I can beat this giant
who *dares* to challenge the power of God!"

David looked straight at Goliath.
He was not afraid.

"God will help me win this battle
for His glory
and keep God's people safe."

So David took his shepherd's staff in his hand
and picked out five smooth stones
for his shepherd's pouch.

One

Two

Three

Four

Five

Then David walked straight up to the giant.

"I come to fight in the name
of the Lord of hosts,
the God of all!
I will strike you down,
but it is God
who defeats you today!"

"No one can beat me,"
roared Goliath.
"Just try it and you'll see!"

David slipped a stone into his mighty sling.

Around and around and around
the sling and stone circled above the shepherd boy.

Whizzzz!
Pop!
Ooooph!
Thud.

The rock hit Goliath's head
and that giant warrior
fell down

dead.

The enemy army shook with fear.
They turned around . . .
and fled!

"Hooray! Hooray! Hip—hip—hooray!"
God's people rejoiced at David's faith
and at God's salvation.

Years later, God chose David to become the king.
Instead of shepherding sheep,
he now shepherded God's people.

David loved to **help** them,
care for them,
guide them,
and keep them **safe**.

Yes, David was
a good shepherd.
And, by faith, David became
a very good king.

FAMILY TALK

Faith Foundation:

God Fights Our Battles

Key Verse

The LORD can save without sword or spear, because the LORD determines every battle's outcome.

1 Samuel 17:47

David was a good shepherd, and a good soldier. Not because he was the biggest or strongest—but because he had faith that God would fight his battles with him.

Like David, we all have a battle to fight. It is a battle against sin. Sin is when we disobey God. The struggle may be hard, but we can know beyond a doubt that God will fight our battles with us. We are not strong enough to stop sinning on our own, but God can help us every day. Pray for faith like David's. Ask God for strength and He will help you choose what is right.

The Promised One came and fought the biggest battle *for* us. He won the victory!

Keep reading to hear more about Him.

What would you have yelled at Goliath before you threw the stone?

How could David be so brave?

FAMILY FUN

Rock Critter Fun

Option #1

Let's have some fun with David's five smooth stones. Let's make Rock Critters. Gather several smooth stones and art supplies. Using your imagination as your guide, make each stone into a little, cheerful critter. Get creative! Use or make googlies for eyes, yarn for hair, mini-marshmallows for feet, or pipe cleaners for arms or antennae! Use your Rock Critters as paperweights, or line them up on a windowsill or shelf. There is no limit to the number of cute critters you can make with David's stones.

Option #2

Draw a picture of David and Goliath in battle. Whiz! Pop! Oomph! Thud! Add this picture to your Bible Story Binder.

THE HERO QUEEN

Esther—Esther 1–10

Do you have a real-life hero?
Someone brave enough and strong enough
to help you when you need it?

Well, this is a story about a hero like that.
A hero from God's people and for God's people.
A brave and beautiful Bible hero named
Esther.

The name Esther means "star."
And that is just what Esther was like.
A beautiful star!

She had a beautiful face,
beautiful hair,
beautiful eyes, and a beautiful smile.

But her outer beauty was not the
most beautiful
part of Esther.
She was even more beautiful
on the inside!

She was loving,
patient,
and respectful.
But, most beautiful of all,
Esther had great
faith in God.

The king noticed Esther's beauty!
He fell in love with her
and made her his queen.

The king and Esther were happy.

But the king had a helper who was not happy.
He was not a hero.

Haman was mean.
Haman was mad.
"I hate God's people," Haman sneered.

So Haman devised a destructive plan
to hurt God's people.

Bad, bad, Haman.

But don't worry,
God was at work
bringing about a special plan for Esther.

Queen Esther heard of Haman's bad plan.

What should I do?
she wondered, and wept.
How can I help God's people?

I must ask the king for help,
she decided.
But anyone who comes before the king uninvited
will be punished!
Oh, what should I do?

What would you do?

Well, Esther wasn't any ordinary queen.
Esther was a hero.
Her beautiful faith in God
gave her the bravery
to go before the king uninvited.

You see,
God was at work,
and His special plan was about to unfold!

Esther walked slowly
into the royal throne room.
She bowed deeply
in respect.
She looked at the king
with love.
And she patiently waited
for him to speak.

Everyone stopped and stared.

"Who is this?
Who dares to break the rules
and come before the king?"
whispered a servant.

Esther held her breath.

But then the king paused
and looked up.
He saw his beautiful queen standing before him.

"Oh, it is you, my love.
Don't be afraid.
Tell me your request."

Esther breathed a sigh of relief.

She invited the king to a banquet and said,

"Please save God's people!
Please save my people!
Please, please, stop Haman's hurtful plan
and save me!"

The king did all that his brave queen asked,
and Haman was taken away.

Queen Esther's
bravery
and her beautiful faith in God
were part of God's plan to save His people!

God's people rejoiced!
"Hooray! Praise God!"

They shouted and danced with joy
because now they knew
God was at work
bringing about His special plan for His people.

"We are safe!" they cried.
"Oh, yes. Thank you God. We are safe!"

And they were.

FAMILY TALK

Faith Foundation:
God Is Always at Work

 A person may plan his own journey,
but the LORD directs his steps.
Proverbs 16:9

God is always at work.

When Esther was chosen to be queen,
when Esther learned of Haman's bad plan,
when Esther bravely asked the king for help,
she couldn't see God at work.

But He was. God was directing every event . . . every step.
God is always at work, my friend; bringing about His good
and loving plan. We may not always be able to see God working,
but we can trust that God has a good plan. Even when things
are sad or bad, God is always at work to bring about His good
plan in our lives. And God never stopped moving and working
to bring about His good plan of salvation through the Promised
One. Through the many years since His promise, He was always
at work, keeping His promise—He brought us a Savior from sin!

Do you think it would be fun to be a king or queen?
Would you be brave enough to go before the king?

FAMILY FUN

A Royal Crown

 Option #1 Let's make a royal crown for you. First, measure around your head with a string. Add at least four inches for taping or stapling the crown together. On stiff paper draw a crown. Cut it out and decorate it with markers, stickers, jewels, or sparkles. You can even use gumdrops or candy. Tape or staple the ends together, dress up like a king or queen, and look into the mirror. Wow! You look regal!

Option #2 Draw a picture of Esther in her royal robes and crown. Add this picture to your Bible Story Binder.

SINGING PSALMS

Psalms 1–150

Do you remember the story of David and Goliath?
God's servant David was a very good shepherd
and a very good king.
But, can you guess what else
King David was good at?
Writing!

King David wrote many beautiful and powerful
prayers and praises to God.

You can read them in a book of the Bible called
Psalms.

David loved to pray.
And just like David, we can pray to God
anytime,
from anywhere,
about anything.

And David loved to praise.
And just like David, we can praise God for

who He is,
what He has promised,
and all He has done for us.

It is good and right for us
to lift up prayers and praises to our God.
And God hears us. Yes,

God loves to listen.

In fact, one of David's psalms says:
**"I love the LORD because
he hears my voice" (Ps. 116:1).**

Which of these psalms are your favorites?

This is the day the LORD has made,
Let's rejoice and be glad today!

Psalm 118:24

I look up toward the mountains
Where can I find help?
My help comes from the LORD,
the maker of heaven and earth.

Psalm 121:1

Give thanks to the LORD, because he is good,
because his mercy endures forever.

Psalm 118:1

Hallelujah!

Praise the LORD from the heavens.
Praise him in the heights above.
Praise him, all his angels.
Praise him, his entire heavenly army.
Praise him, sun and moon.
Praise him, all shining stars.
Praise him, you highest heaven
   and the water above the sky.
Let them praise the name of the LORD.

Psalm 148:1–5

You alone created my inner being.
You knitted me together inside my mother.
I will give thanks to you
    because I have been so amazingly and miraculously made.
        Your works are miraculous, and my soul is fully aware
    of this.

Psalm 139:13–14

Praise the LORD, my soul,
    and never forget all the good he has done;
        He is the one who forgives all your sins,
            the one who heals all your diseases,
            the one who rescues your life from the pit,
            the one who crowns you with mercy and compassion,
            the one who fills your life with blessings
                so that you become young again like an eagle.

Psalm 103:2–5

Yes, it is good and right to lift up prayers and
praises to God.
Praise Him! Praise Him!
Praise the Lord!

FAMILY TALK

Faith Foundation:
God Is Worthy of Praise

Sing to the LORD! Praise his name!
Day after day announce that the LORD saves
his people.

Psalm 96:2

God, you are awesome!
God, you are wonderful!
God, you are big and loving and kind!
God, help me.
God, watch over me and guide me.
God, thank you for my family and friends and home.
These are some praises and prayers you can lift up to God, right here and right now. Anytime . . . all the time, is a good time to talk to God. God desires our prayers and deserves our praises because He is the one true God. And He has done great things for us—like keeping His promise for a Savior!

Do you think God deserves our praises? Why?

What do you want to pray about today?

How many things can you think of to be thankful for?

FAMILY FUN

Delicious Words of Praise!

  Option #1 Using premade cookie or bread dough, let's praise God. Roll out strips, not too thin, and form them into praise words on a lightly greased cookie sheet. Follow package directions and bake. Eat them as you praise the Lord together. Yum! You can also make praise words out of yarn or rope or . . .

Suggested Words:
Joy
Hallelujah
Jesus
Lord
Promise

Option #2 Write your own psalm praising God for who He is and all He has done for you. Say or write a prayer of thanksgiving to God.

Option #3 Draw a beautiful picture of yourself praising God, showing your hands held high in the air. Add this picture to your Bible Story Binder.

WAY OF WISDOM

Proverbs 1–31

Wisdom is knowing the right thing to do and having the strength to do it.

Did you know there is an entire book of the Bible devoted to wisdom?

It is called the book of Proverbs.

It tells us how to obey our parents.
It tells us how to choose good friends.
It tells us how to respect, honor, and love God.

God longs for His people to live with wisdom.
Oh, yes!

To know what is right.
To know what is best.

And He will give us the strength
to choose wisdom.

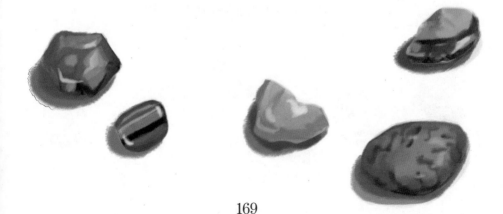

God says wisdom is worth more
than silver or gold.

Worth more than precious diamonds or pearls.

Worth more than all the treasures of the world.

Wow!

Imagine a heaping pile of treasures
reaching over your head!

Here are a few of those precious jewels of wisdom.

A happy proverb:
**"A joyful heart
makes a cheerful face." (15:13)**

A teaching proverb:
**"The fear of the Lord
is the beginning of wisdom.
The knowledge of the Holy One
is understanding." (9:10)**

A warning proverb:
**"A fool's mouth is his ruin.
His lips are a trap to his soul." (18:7)**

A yummy proverb:
**"Pleasant words are like
honey from a honeycomb—
sweet to the spirit and
healthy for the body." (16:24)**

An encouraging proverb:
**"Every word of God has proven to be true.
He is a shield to those who come to him
for protection." (30:5)**

An obedience proverb:
**"Carefully walk a straight path
and all your ways will be secure.
Do not lean to the right or to the left.
Walk away from evil." (4:26–27)**

Yes, God wants us to listen,
because He is the source of all wisdom.
We will be blessed if we live according
to His Word.

Here is a final proverb:
"Cherish wisdom.
It will raise you up.
It will bring you honor when you embrace it.
It will give you a
graceful garland for your head.
It will hand you a beautiful crown." (4:8–9)

FAMILY TALK

Faith Foundation:

God's Way Is Wise

 Key Verse Wisdom is more precious than jewels,
and all your desires cannot equal it.
Proverbs 3:15

The Bible calls the Promised One, the "Wisdom of God."
And He is.

That is because He is right.

He is best.

And He gives us the faith to believe in Him.

What a wonderful promise of God.

He promises wisdom to those who seek it.

And faith to those who long for it.

Yes. The Promised One came to be God's wisdom for us . . .

The right and best choice for a blessed life.

He is worth more than precious jewels.

He is better than all your deepest desires.

"He is Christ, God's power and God's wisdom" (1 Cor. 1:24).

What is your favorite proverb? Why?

FAMILY FUN

Book of Proverbs

Option #1

Make your own book of God's Proverbs. Read through the book and choose four proverbs you want to learn. Illustrate each proverb and staple them together to make a book. Type, cut, and paste the proverb on the bottom of each page. Sit down, cuddle up, and read it together!

Option #2

Trace around your foot to make a footprint pattern. Cut out many footprints. Write your favorite proverbs on each one. To remind you to walk a straight and wise path, tape your footprints to the floor and step on each one.

Option #3

Draw a beautiful picture of a giant jewel. God says that wisdom is worth more than all the treasure in the world.

Add this picture to your Bible Story Binder.

GOD'S PROPHETS

Isaiah—Malachi

Can you believe that many times
God's people turned away?

They turned away from
God's Ten Commandments.
They turned away from
God's ways and words of wisdom.
They turned away from hope in the Promised One.
In fact, they turned away from God altogether.

So, God sent His people
special messengers, called
prophets.

These prophets gave God's people
important messages and warnings:
Turn back to God!
Turn back to God's commandments!
Turn back to hope in
the Promised One!

Each prophet gave hints about the Promised One,
our Savior,
who saves us from our sin.

Isaiah called the Promised One
our Suffering Servant.
Ezekiel announced Him as
our King who reigns in glory.
Daniel said He stands beside us in fiery troubles.

Hosea declared the Promised One
is our forever love.
Joel told He baptizes us with the Holy Spirit.
Micah prophesied He is our peace.

Jonah foreshadowed the Promised One
in the deep for three days, rising in victory.
Zephaniah wrote He is a mighty warrior
coming to save us.

All the prophets proclaimed that

the Promised One is our Savior,
the only one who can take away our sin,
so we can live joyfully with God forever!

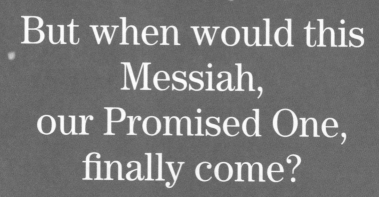

But when would this Messiah, our Promised One, finally come?

The world wondered.

They waited.

And waited.

And waited.

In hope, they waited and wondered and believed:
God's Promised One, our Savior, is coming!

FAMILY TALK

Faith Foundation:

God Promises a Savior from Sin

Key Verse

A child will be born for us.
A son will be given to us.
    The government will rest on his shoulders.
He will be named:
    Wonderful Counselor,
    Mighty God,
    Everlasting Father,
    Prince of Peace.

Isaiah 9:6

The word *prophet* means "someone who sees." Each prophet of God could see only one tiny puzzle piece of God's plan for sending the Promised One. Here are some of the puzzle pieces the prophets told about the Promised One:

Born in Bethlehem
Named Immanuel
Performs Miracles
Teaches in Parables

Rides on a Donkey
Gives His Life
Ascends to heaven

What is your favorite prophecy of the Promised One? They all came true!

The prophets said the Promised One was coming—are you ready to meet Him?

FAMILY FUN

Your Life's Puzzle—A Beautiful Work of Art

 Do you like puzzles? I do! Take a photo of your family or yourself and cut it into a crazy puzzle with swervy, curvy lines. Can you tell what the picture is by looking at only one piece? Have everyone put their puzzle together and see how fast they can complete it.

God always has a plan. Nothing ever happens in your life without Him knowing all about it. Every day is one little piece of the puzzle. Some days are bright red and cheery yellow; some days are dark blue with hints of gray. And when all the pieces of your life are put together, God will make sure it forms a beautiful work of art.

 Draw a beautiful picture of the Promised One as a King in royal robes, holding a jeweled scepter. Don't forget His golden crown! Add this picture to your Bible Story Binder.

NEW
TESTAMENT

THE PROMISE COMES

Christmas—Luke 2:1–20

The time was now.
The time was here.
The time had come for the

Promised One

to appear!

God marked this awesome
and amazing birth
with a special sign hanging in the dark night sky.

A giant,
glorious,
twinkling
star
silently shone a brilliant bright light.

Wow!
What an
incredible sight.

Way, way down below God's wonderful star
was a little town called Bethlehem.

And way, way within that tiny town
was a little bustling inn.

And way, way behind that full and noisy inn
was a little stable packed with animals.

And way, way inside this humble stable shed
was a little manger filled with hay.

And inside that manger
a baby lay
sleeping softly in the silvery light
of God's special star.

Mary smiled at her sweet child.
Joseph looked on Him with love.

The Promised One had arrived!

The Son of God was born.

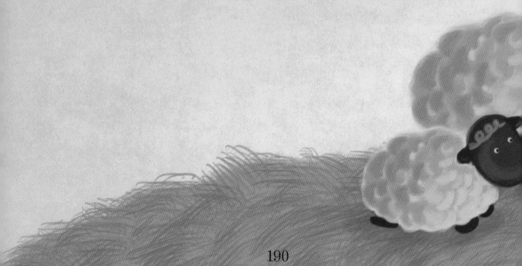

And His name is
Jesus.
Immanuel.
God with Us.
And that is who He is.

Out in the fields
shepherds watched over their sheep.
FLASH!

A bright light filled the night sky.
The glory of God surrounded the shepherds.

An angel stood before the frightened shepherds
and proclaimed,

"I bring you good news!
The Promised One
the Savior
Christ the Lord
is born today!"

A multitude of angels appeared and sang praises,
"Glory to God in the highest heaven!"

And so the shepherds ran to the town,
ran to the stable,
ran to the manger where their Savior was sleeping.

Holding their breath, the shepherds
knelt before baby Jesus.
In awe, they watched Him sleep.
And they knew that He had come
for them.

And as the shepherds hurried back toward the fields,
they rejoiced throughout the streets of the town
and gave glory to God
for the greatest gift ever given . . .

Jesus
the
Promised One.

But the shepherds weren't the only ones
who came to see the newborn
King of Kings
and Lord of Lords.

Wise men from the East
saw the star sparkle high in the sky.
Overwhelmed with joy,
they followed it in faith.

Miles and miles
over deserts and mountains
they traveled long months and days
to bring the Promised One their praise
and precious gifts of

gold

frankincense

myrrh.

Arriving in Bethlehem,
the wise men fell on their faces
in worship
and laid their treasure chests before baby Jesus.

You see,
Jesus came for everyone.
For the poor shepherds, the rich wise men,
for people from every nation and every tribe,
for your neighbors and your family,
for you and for me.
Yes,
"God loved the world this way:
He gave his only Son so that everyone
who believes in him
will not die but will have eternal life" (John 3:16).

And now we see,
God keeps His promises.
He sent the One, His only Son,
who will take away our sin
so we can live joyfully with God forever.

FAMILY TALK

Faith Foundation:

Jesus Is the Promised One

"She will give birth to a son, and you will name him Jesus (He Saves), because he will save his people from their sins." All this happened so that what the Lord had spoken through the prophet came true: . . . "they will name him Immanuel," which means "God is with us."

Matthew 1:21–23

Finally! The Promised One was here. And He came as a beautiful baby boy in a humble stable of hay. An angel announcing His arrival gave Him two very important names.

Jesus. This name means "He Saves." And it's true—He does save us. Jesus saves us from the punishment of sin and gives us eternal life with God.

Immanuel. This name means "God with us." And that is true too. You see, Jesus is not an ordinary little baby boy. The Promised One is the Son of God. By nature, He is God Himself!

Which of His names do you like best? Why?

What gift would you give to baby Jesus?

Describe what you think the star looked like.

FAMILY FUN

The Best Present Ever

 The best present that was ever given is Jesus, God's Son. Find or make a picture of baby Jesus or use a nativity. Carefully wrap it in beautiful tissue paper and put it in a box. Decorate the box or wrap it like a lovely Christmas present. Set the gift in a special place in your home. Tomorrow, open the gift and set Jesus where you will see Him often. Write a prayer of praise to God for sending us His Son, Jesus . . . the best present ever!

 Act out the Christmas story, or sing a few of your favorite Christmas carols.

Draw a beautiful picture of the Christmas star. Include an angel singing to the shepherds, "Gloria!" Add this picture to your Bible Story Binder.

BEHOLD, THE LAMB!

John the Baptist—Matthew 3:1–17;
Mark 1:1–13; Luke 3:1–22; John 1:19–34

John the Baptist
was a wild man
with a wonderful mission.

He ate lunches of locusts and wild honey.
He wore clothes of camel hair and stood in the dry
desert proclaiming,

"Prepare your hearts for the Promised One!"

The people came to hear.
They confessed and turned away from their sin.

They walked into the flowing water
of the Jordan River and were
baptized.

The people understood that sin must be punished.
So they told God they were sorry
and longed for salvation.

Where is the Promised One?
When will He come?
They waited and wondered.

Only He can take away our sin forever!

And then, one wonderful day,
Jesus came down to the river.

"Behold!"

John the Baptist shouted,
pointing to Jesus,

"The Lamb of God
who takes away
the sin of the world!"

Yes, John knew that Jesus was the Promised One.
He knew that Jesus was the only one
who could take away people's sins.

The people watched,
astonished,
as Jesus stepped into the water to be baptized.

"How can I baptize you?"
John the Baptist asked.
"You have no sin!
You have lived a perfect life."

But Jesus insisted.

"Let it be so."

So John dunked Jesus down under the deep water.
Jesus came up quickly
and something amazing happened . . .

John the Baptist
gasped
as he looked into the sky!

The heavens opened, the clouds rolled back,
and the Spirit of God
came down on Jesus like a dove.

"You are my beloved Son!"
God's voice thundered.
"In you, I am well pleased."

Many people began to follow Jesus that day.
He traveled from town to town
city to city
teaching the crowds
about God
and His love
and His Kingdom.

Jesus healed many sicknesses!
He performed many miracles!
He taught wondrous and amazing truths!

All to show the world that:

**Jesus alone is God's Promised One,
Jesus alone is the Savior from our sin,
Jesus alone is our gentle and loving Lord.**

FAMILY TALK

Faith Foundation:

Jesus Is the Lamb of God

When John the Baptist yelled out, "Look! This is the Lamb of God!" he proclaimed for all to hear that Jesus is the Promised One. He encouraged people to follow Jesus and listen to His teachings and learn all about God's wonderful plan of salvation.

You see, before Jesus came, people used to sacrifice a lamb in the temple as they asked God to forgive them for their sin. But now, Jesus came to be that lamb for us forever.

Yes, Jesus is God's Lamb . . . who takes away the sin of the world!

Have you ever seen anyone be baptized? Tell me about it. What did you like best about this story?

FAMILY FUN

 Honey-Colored Locust Leg Cookies!

Option #1

Remember how John the Baptist ate honey and locusts?
Let's make a batch of honey-colored locust legs.

6 oz. chow mein noodles
6 oz. butterscotch chips
¼ cup peanut butter
Melt the butterscotch chips in a microwave bowl.
Add the peanut butter and stir until smooth.
Stir in the chow mein noodles
Drop by spoonfuls on wax paper.
Chill in the refrigerator for 15 minutes to set.
Open wide . . . and eat those locust legs.

Crunch! Munch!

Option #2

Draw a picture of the Holy Spirit descending like a dove onto Jesus. Wow! Add this picture to your Bible Story Binder.

BLIND FAITH

A Miracle—Matthew 20:29–34; Mark 10:46–52; Luke 18:35–43

Bartimaeus was a blind man.
He lived in darkness,
begged for bread,
and listened as life passed him by.

Bartimaeus had never seen a sunset.
Never studied a wildflower.
Never looked long on the smiling faces
of family and friends.

No.
Bartimaeus spent his days
sitting on the side of the busy city streets
holding out his cup for coins
and listening to tiny bits of conversations
as people walked by.

Yes, people passed by
as Bartimaeus sat on the sidelines of life.
They talked about the weather,
about their children,
about their lives full of activity and work and fun—
things Bartimaeus could never have.

But today something was different.
Today the people talked of only one thing.
The people talked about Jesus.

"He'll be passing by soon . . ."
"Jesus, the Promised One!"
"He is simply amazing!"

Jesus . . .

Oh, yes! Bartimaeus had heard that name before.

I've heard many people talk about Jesus
thought Bartimaeus.
He teaches, He preaches, and some say . . .
He does miracles!

Now, Bartimaeus may have been a blind man,
but he could clearly see the truth:

Jesus is
the Promised One.

Maybe . . .
thought Bartimaeus,
just maybe God's Promised One
knows *me,*
loves *me,*
and **longs to help** *me.*

Yes, Jesus is my only hope.

"There He is!" someone shouted.

The voices of the crowd rolled and thundered as
they cried out to Jesus,
but one voice could be heard above the rest.

"Jesus! Have mercy on me!"

Bartimaeus shouted with all his strength
as he wandered into the crowd.
His arms stretched out
into the darkness around him.
Bartimaeus became lost in the swirl of bodies.
He no longer knew which direction he came from
or which direction to go to find the man of his hope:
Jesus.

"Jesus! Promised One!
Have mercy on me!"

"Be still blind man!" said the crowd.
But Bartimaeus would not be still.

"Promised One!"
he shouted even louder,
"Please have mercy!"

Then, Bartimaeus heard a gentle voice.
Jesus spoke:
"What is it you want?"

"Lord," said blind Bartimaeus, "I want to see."

Now, you see, Jesus **knew** Bartimaeus.
Jesus **loved** Bartimaeus.
And Jesus **longed to help** Bartimaeus.

And when Jesus looked into the dark eyes
of blind Bartimaeus, He found
faith.

Bartimaeus closed his eyes.
He was a blind beggar
tired and worn
helpless and hopeless.

But when Bartimaeus opened his eyes,
he was healed!

He was a new man, now blinded by bright light.

And his first sight was the most beautiful sight
he would ever see . . .
Not a sunset glowing in glory,
not a field full of wildflowers,
not even the smiling faces of family and friends.

He saw the face
of His Savior.

"I can see . . . I can see."
Bartimaeus whispered,
"Thank you, Jesus."

And as Bartimaeus's eyes
filled with the thankful tears of a humble son,
the eyes of Jesus, the Promised One,
filled with the joy of a loving Father.

FAMILY TALK

Faith Foundation:

Jesus Has Power over Sickness

A large crowd came to him, bringing with them the lame, blind, disabled, those unable to talk, and many others. They laid them at his feet, and he cured them. The crowd was amazed to see mute people talking, the disabled cured, the lame walking, and the blind seeing. So they praised the God of Israel.

Matthew 15:30–31

Jesus was filled with compassion for those who were hurting, and He had great power to heal them. These miracles of healing revealed the heart of the Promised One. Jesus's humility, mercy, and love filled Him with an overwhelming desire to help those who were in need.

And these healings proved to everyone who Jesus was: the Promised One, God's Son, our Savior from sin. Every blind man that He made to see, every lame man He made to walk, every sick man and woman who was healed, shouted out to the multitudes: "This is God's Promised One! He is God's Son! He has authority over all things!"

Do you think Jesus feels compassion for you when you hurt? What is your favorite part of this Bible story?

FAMILY FUN

Blindfolded Lunch

Blindfold everyone. On a plastic tablecloth, eat your breakfast, lunch, or a snack without using your eyes. If you have trouble, one adult can take off his or her blindfold and give verbal directions to everyone else. No peeking! Discuss what it feels like to be blind, and what you would do if Jesus had healed you like Bartimaeus.

Draw a beautiful picture of Jesus's face. Add this picture to your Bible Story Binder.

LAZARUS LIVES

A Miracle—John 11:1–44

Do you have a good friend?
Someone who makes you feel warm
and laugh out loud?

Jesus did.

He had a very good friend named Lazarus.

But one day, something sad happened.
Lazarus got sick and died.

His sister Mary was sad.
His sister Martha was sad.
His friends and his neighbors were all so very sad.

And Jesus was sad too.
But Jesus knew that God had a plan
for His glory.

Four days after Lazarus died,
Jesus came to see Mary and Martha.

"Oh, Lord,"
they said,
"If you had been here, Lazarus would not have died.
You could have healed him."

Jesus said to them,
**"I am the resurrection and the life!
He who believes in me will never die.
Do you believe this?"**

"Yes, we believe.
You are the Promised One!"
They led Jesus to the tomb . . .
and then . . .

Jesus wept.

His tears fell like raindrops in a dark storm.

Suddenly, Jesus stopped crying.

"Now you will see the glory of God!"

Jesus looked up,
wiped away his wet tears,
and lifted His hands high toward heaven.

"Father, thank you. Let these people believe
that You sent Me!"

The crowd hushed to hear
as Jesus talked to His heavenly Father.

Looking at the tomb,
Jesus commanded in a loud voice,

"Lazarus, come out!"

For a moment, nothing happened.
Everything and everyone was silent and still.
Mary and Martha held their breath
waiting . . . wondering . . . hoping . . .

And then . . .
Rustle—Rustle—Rustle

Out of the tomb walked Lazarus
still wrapped in his burial cloths.

He was alive!

"Unwrap him. Free him."
Jesus smiled as He spoke.

Everyone jumped for joy!
Shouts of happiness echoed
off the surrounding hills.

"He's alive! He's alive! Lazarus is alive!
It's a miracle!"

And Jesus, thankful to have Lazarus at His side,
threw His arms around His friend,
embraced him,
and laughed.

FAMILY TALK

Faith Foundation:

Jesus Has Power over Death

Jesus said to her, "I am the one who brings people back to life, and I am life itself. Those who believe in me will live even if they die. Everyone who lives and believes in me will never die. Do you believe that?"

John 11:25–26

Jesus loved Lazarus and raised him from the dead. Yes, Jesus has power over death. If we put our faith in the Promised One, we will receive eternal life as a free gift. And someday, because of Jesus, God will raise us from the dead and take us up to heaven to live with Him forever.

Jesus proclaimed that He is the life. And He longs to give new life to each one of us—to forgive us our sin and renew our hearts to be at peace with God. Yes, Jesus is Life!

What is your favorite part of this Bible story?
In this story, Jesus feels sad. What makes you feel sad?
What helps you feel happy again?

FAMILY FUN

Family Friendship Chain

Option #1

How many friends do you have? Let's make a l-o-n-g family friendship chain. Cut many strips of colored paper about 1 inch wide and 8½ inches long. Using a colored or black marker, write the name of one special friend on each strip of paper. Decorate each strip if you like. Firmly tape or staple each strip into a loop. Slip another strip through loop one and tape its ends together to form a second loop. Add as many friends and loops as you can. How long can you make your friendship chain? Hang up your chain. Keep adding loops as you remember more friends. Pastor, neighbor, teacher. Don't forget each other.

Option #2

Draw a picture, write a note, call, or email friends to tell them how special they are to you.

Option #3

Draw a beautiful picture of you with all your friends. Remember, Jesus is your friend too! Add this picture to your Bible Story Binder.

PEACE IN THE STORM

A Miracle—Matthew 8:23–27; Mark 4:35–41; Luke 8:22–25

Have you ever gone on a boat ride?
It's fun!

The breeze blows on your face,
and tiny waves splash drops of water
on your skin.

One time, Jesus told his twelve closest friends,
called disciples,
"Let's go on a boat ride
across the still, smooth sea."

246

Leaving the crowds, Jesus and His disciples
climbed into the boat.

The disciples began to row.
Pull
Pull
Pull
And Jesus, tired from teaching,
lay down on a cushion and quickly
fell asleep.

Suddenly, a ferocious storm started!

Gentle breezes became fierce gusts of wind.
Tiny waves became huge walls of water
that broke over the boat and

filled

it

up!

"We are shivering,"
the disciples cried out in fear!

They rowed harder.
Pull
Pull
Pull
But they could not outrun the fierce storm.

"We are scared,"
the terrified disciples cried out!

They rowed as hard as they could.
Pull
Pull
Pull

But they could not reach safety on the other shore.

"We are sinking!"
the men shouted,
"Jesus! Jesus, save us!"

Jesus woke up.

He was **not shivering** from fear.
He was **not scared** of the storm.
His trust in God, His Father,
was **not sinking** with the boat.

"Hush. Be still."

With Jesus's words, the wind died down.
The sea hushed to silence.
And everything became
perfectly calm.

The disciples were amazed.
Now dripping wet in the sunshine,
they could hardly believe what just happened.

They asked one another,
"Who is Jesus,
that even the wind and waves obey Him?"

That is an important question for all of us.

Who is Jesus?

The Bible tells us:
He is the Son of God.
He is the Promised One.
He is the Savior who will take away our sin
so we can live joyfully with God forever!

Yes, that is who Jesus is!

FAMILY TALK

 Faith Foundation:

Jesus Has Power over Creation

Frightened and amazed, they asked each other, "Who is this man? He gives orders to the wind and the water, and they obey him!"

Luke 8:25

Who is Jesus that He has power over the storm? Yes, who is this man? He is God Himself. The Promised One. Our Savior.

We all have storms or problems in our lives. Troubles can happen that make us sad or scared. But in this story Jesus shows us He has power over every storm or problem that comes our way. We can trust completely in God's care and compassion for us. When we are afraid, we can think of Jesus calming the winds and the waves and believe that Jesus has power over our storm too. Yes, God is in control and we can always find hope in Him.

Who is Jesus to you?

What storms or problems make you sad or scared?

Do you believe God has power over these things?

Be sure to pray. Ask God to give you a calm peace in your heart.

FAMILY FUN

"Peace! Be Still!"

Option #1

Let's act out Jesus calming the storm. Set up pillows, chairs, or boxes to make the outline of a boat. Everyone get into the boat and sit on the floor. Take turns playing Jesus and place a pillow in the front for Jesus to sleep on. Everyone else row—row—row the boat. Swooosh! Whooosh! Here comes the storm. Rock this way and that way and this way and that way. Shield your faces from the splashing waves. Cry out to Jesus! Now, the person playing Jesus will stand up and calm the storm. "Peace! Be Still." It's a miracle! Row, row, row to the other shore. Choose a new person to play "Jesus" and repeat.

Option #2

Draw a picture of Jesus calming the storm. Add this picture to your Bible Story Binder.

LOST AND FOUND

A Parable—Luke 15:3–7

Jesus, the Promised One, is a
master storyteller.

Crowds gathered outside of town.
Men, Women, Girls, Boys
Rich, Poor, Young, Old
Healthy, Sick, Happy, Sad
all came together to listen and learn from Jesus.
There was no place Jesus would rather be
than speaking to the crowds,
tenderly teaching them the truth about God and
His plan of salvation.

The people hushed
and heard every word of hope . . .
every word of the Promised One
they had waited for.
Here is one of the stories Jesus told . . .

A flock of sheep grazed lazily
in their fine green fields.
Baa . . .
Baa . . .
Baa . . .

The Good Shepherd silently sat nearby
joyfully looking over the little lambs
He loved.

"I know and adore every one of my sheep,"
said the Shepherd.

But one little sheep
without wisdom wandered away . . .
far, far away from the flock and became

lost.

Lost and lonely.

When the Good Shepherd saw
that the little lamb was lost,
He quickly put on His cloak,
grabbed His shepherd's staff,
and left to find His precious one.

He searched down low in the deep, dark valleys.
He searched wide, over the flat, open plains.
He searched high, on the steep, jagged hills.
He even climbed

up

up

up

to the tip-top of the mountain peaks.

The Good Shepherd never gave up.

Night came, and with it came cold darkness.

The little lamb was scared.

Baa . . .

Baa . . .

Baa . . .

A quiet, tiny voice
reached the Good Shepherd's ears.

Baa . . .

Baa . . .

Baa . . .

The Good Shepherd raced to the edge of a cliff
and looked down the steep ledge.

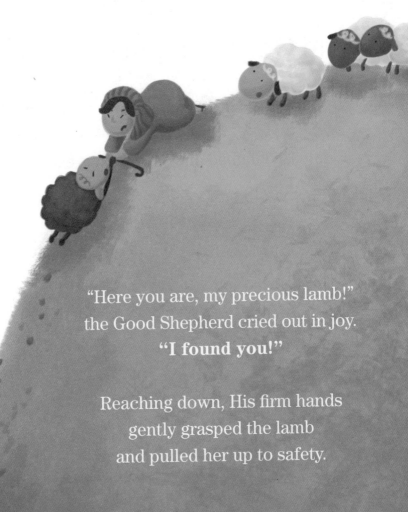

"Here you are, my precious lamb!"
the Good Shepherd cried out in joy.
"I found you!"

Reaching down, His firm hands
gently grasped the lamb
and pulled her up to safety.

The Good Shepherd rejoiced!

He carried the little lamb on His strong shoulders
all the way home
while He laughed and sang with great gladness.

**"My sheep was lost,
but I have found the one I love!"**

Oh, yes. Wasn't Jesus a great storyteller?

FAMILY TALK

Faith Foundation:

Jesus Teaches Truth: Jesus Is Your Good Shepherd

Key Verse

Indeed, the Son of Man (Jesus) has come to seek and to save people who are lost.

Luke 19:10

Who do you think is the lost lamb? It's you! It's true!

Just like sheep, we have all wandered away from God. You are the little lamb that Jesus has found and rejoices over. Jesus said, "I am the Good Shepherd. I know my sheep. I will give my life for my sheep." Yes, Jesus is your good and loving Shepherd. He even knows your name. He knows everything about you. Yes, He knows you and loves you . . . abundantly.

And Jesus gave His life for you. How? Keep reading to find out. You'll be excited. This story has a most happy ending!

What is your favorite part of the story of the little lost lamb?

Do you like being Jesus's little lamb?

What is the best thing about having a Good Shepherd?

FAMILY FUN

Hide-and-Seek Sheep

Option #1
Take turns being Jesus, the Good Shepherd. The Good Shepherd is "it." All the others are wandering sheep. The Good Shepherd closes his eyes and counts to twenty while all the sheep scatter and hide. Then, the Good Shepherd must find each and every one of his lost sheep. If the Good Shepherd needs help finding you, quietly "baaaaa. . . ." You can also play this game by hiding stuffed animals to search and find.

Option #2
Make a nametag in the shape of a heart or sheep. On it, write "Jesus loves (your name)". Wear it.

Option #3
Draw a picture of the Good Shepherd finding His lost sheep. Add this picture to your Bible Story Binder.

FIRM FOUNDATION

A Parable—Matthew 7:24–29; Luke 6:47–49

Jesus,
the Promised One,

longed for His people not only to hear His words,
but to believe them,
understand them,
and do them.

So, out of His great
love and compassion,
He told the crowds another exciting story.
A story about two men.

Two men building
two houses.

Once there was a man,
a very wise man,
who wanted to build
a big and beautiful house.

He dug a deep hole,

oomph!

and built his house
on top of a strong, secure rock.

It was very hard work.
He was tired and worn out,
but the wise man knew it was important
to have a firm foundation.

"My house is solid and safe,"
the wise man said.

Once there was another man,
a very foolish man,
who also wanted to build
a big and beautiful house.

But he did not want to work hard.
He didn't dig a hole,
yawn . . .
and built his house on the shifting sand.

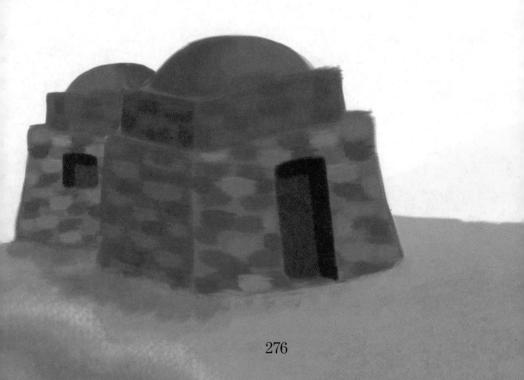

It didn't take much work.
He was lazy and prideful,
because the foolish man didn't care about having a
firm foundation.

"My house is good enough . . ."
the foolish man said.

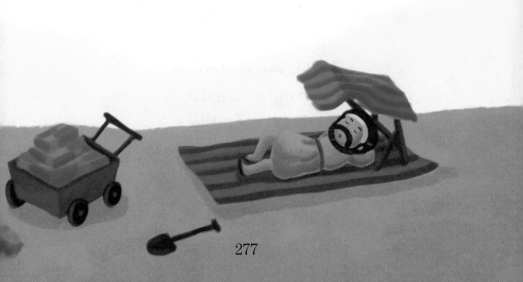

One night . . .

Flash!

Crash!

A violent, rainy, blustery storm
began to blow.

The streams flooded!
Water gushed and rushed toward the two men
sleeping silently in their two houses.

The wise man awoke and watched
as the waves of water crashed against his house.

But his house stood still.
It did not shake.
It did not rattle.
It did not rumble or crumble or roll.

The wise man's house
stood strong
on its firm foundation.

The foolish man awoke and watched
as the waves of water crashed against his house.

But his house did not stand still!
It shook!
It rattled!
It rumbled and crumbled and rolled . . .

and rolled . . .

and rolled . . .

and rolled . . .

and rolled right away!

**The foolish man's house
completely washed away in the waves.**

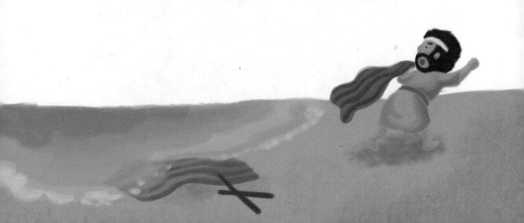

Jesus said,
"Everyone who hears my words
and does them
is like the wise man."

Build your life on Jesus!
Believe in Him and He will be your solid rock.
Yes, Jesus will be your firm foundation forever.

FAMILY TALK

Faith Foundation:

Jesus Teaches Truth: Build Your House on the Rock

Key Verse

Therefore, everyone who hears what I say and obeys it will be like a wise person who built a house on rock.

Matthew 7:24

Our lives are like a house. Every day, our hearts build either a wise, strong life of faith that brings glory to God or a foolish, weak life of unbelief that does not glorify God. Do you want to be like the wise man? I do!

Putting all your faith in Jesus is like laying a good foundation for your whole life—like a solid rock. Jesus Himself is our strong support to help us stand firm through any storm or hard time. Yes, Jesus is our firm foundation! Build your life on the Promised One.

Do you love to listen to Jesus?

Do you want to obey Him?

What kind of house do you want to build?

What kind of life do you want to live?

FAMILY FUN

Building Blocks

Option #1

Pull out your building blocks and make a few houses. First, build your house on a pillow—that is like the shifting sand. How well did it hold up? Now, build your house on the hard, firm floor. That house is much stronger. Just for fun, knock both houses down and build them again.

Option #2

Pretend to have a picnic at the wise man's house to celebrate his firm foundation. Put down a plastic tablecloth on the floor, the lawn, or the patio. Use paper plates and simple fun food. Invite some friends to join you. Yum! Have fun!

Option #3

Draw a beautiful picture of the wise man building his house on the rock of Jesus. Add this picture to your Bible Story Binder.

CHILDREN OF GOD

Jesus Blesses the Children—Matthew 19:13–15;
Mark 10:13–16; Luke 18:15–17

Children loved to be with Jesus.
And Jesus, the Promised One,
loved to be with children.

He loved their smiles.
He loved their games.
He loved their joy
and jokes and silliness.

But do you know what Jesus
loved best about children?
Their simple faith.

Children often believe in Jesus
with all their hearts.

Once, when Jesus was teaching adults,
some children came to see Him.

"Go away!"
the disciples said.
"He is too busy for you."

The children still pushed closer to Jesus,
with hopeful smiles
on their faces.

"Leave the teacher alone,"
the crowds told them.

But Jesus stopped teaching.
He decided to teach the adults a different lesson.

**"Let the little children come to Me.
Let them sit right here . . . on my knee."**

Jesus took the children in His arms
and put His loving hands on their heads
and He blessed them.

"The kingdom of God belongs to children like these."

He proclaimed.

**"Anyone who loves a child in My name
is showing love to Me."**

That is how special children are to our Savior.
Oh, yes. Jesus loves children!

You see, Jesus didn't come to take away only the
sins of grown-ups.

No.

He came for the children of the world.

Him.

Her.

You.

Me.

And the Bible tells us,
everyone who puts all their faith in Jesus,
become children . . .

Yes, children of God!

Girls. Boys. Mommies. Daddies.
Grandmothers. Grandfathers.
If they are nine years old—or ninety-nine years old
they can be children
by simple faith.

Children of God!

FAMILY TALK

Faith Foundation:

Jesus Seeks Simple Faith

 Key Verse   You are all God's children by believing in Christ Jesus.

Galatians 3:26

Children loved to come to Jesus! They ran to Him with great joy. And Jesus loved to have the children come to Him and sit with Him. That is because children are precious. They long to believe the truth. They have humble, simple faith.

The Bible says we become God's children by faith in Jesus. Yes, by humble, simple faith in Jesus Christ, you can become children of God.

And He is such a wonderful Friend and Savior.

What was your favorite part of the story of Jesus and the children?

Aren't you glad Jesus loves little children like you and like me?

What is the best part about being a child? About being a child of God?

FAMILY FUN

 **Bless Me!**

Option #1
Parents, bless your children.
   Put your hand on their heads and pray aloud for God to move in their hearts, to give them faith in Jesus alone, and to guide them into a life that brings Him glory.

Option #2
Isn't it great that Jesus loves little children—like you and like me? Sing the song "Jesus Loves the Little Children" with a voice of praise to the wonderful Promised One who loves children.

Option #3
Draw a picture of a big heart. Then draw yourself and Jesus holding hands inside of the heart. Add this picture to your Bible Story Binder.

HOSANNA!

The Triumphant Entry—Matthew 21:1–11;
Mark 11:1–11; Luke 19:29–44; John 12:12–19

Jesus fixed His eyes on Jerusalem, the holy city,
and rode toward it on a young donkey.

As Jesus got closer and closer to the city,
the crowds grew bigger and bigger.

The prophets long ago foretold this day:
"Here comes your King, gentle,
and seated on a donkey."

The large group of people smiled
and shouted and sang praises
to God and to the Promised One.

"Hosanna! Save us!"
People laughed and danced
as they followed Jesus.
"Hosanna in the highest!"

298

The crowd spread their coats and cloaks
on the dusty ground,
creating a humble royal carpet for Jesus.
Others laid out tall tree branches,
or waved them in the air in honor and praise.

A little boy waved a palm branch.
A little girl clapped her hands.
And Jesus smiled at them in love.

Peace in heaven!
Glory in the highest!

Behind Him and before Him, the crowd ushered
Jesus into Jerusalem.
Jesus liked His triumphant entry.

He knew it was right to give Him honor and praise.
He knew He was about to fulfill
God's important promise.
And Jesus knew
He was about to take away our sin,
so we can live joyfully with God forever.

FAMILY TALK

Faith Foundation:

Jesus Is King

Key Verse

Some of the Pharisees in the crowd said to Jesus, "Teacher tell your disciples to be quiet." Jesus replied, "I can guarantee that if they are quiet, the stones will cry out.

Luke 19:39–40

Jesus is the King!

It was good and right to praise Jesus as the King. Jesus said that if the people had stopped praising Him, the very rocks would begin to cry out in praise! Yes, oh yes! Praise Jesus! The King of Kings and Lord of Lords.

We enter the kingdom of heaven by repentance and faith. And we, His children, receive all the benefits of His reign: forgiveness, joy, and the ability to know and enjoy God for all eternity. Praise God! Jesus is King!

What was your favorite part of the triumphal entry?
Is Jesus King of your life?
How loud can you shout "Hosanna!"? Try it.

FAMILY FUN

A Triumphant Parade

Option #1

Jesus came into Jerusalem in a loud parade on Palm Sunday. Let's have a triumphant entry right here—right now.

Start by making some palm branches to wave. Cut them out of green construction paper. Then, dress up for your wonderful parade using bathrobes, scarves, hats, etc. Using coats, towels, and pillowcases, lay out your cloaks before Jesus. Wave your palm branches. Shout out your praises to God! Choose another Jesus and do it again. Who wants to be the donkey?

Option #2

Draw a picture of your favorite part of Palm Sunday. Add this picture to your Bible Story Binder.

GOOD, GOOD NEWS

Crucifixion and Easter—Matthew 27:31–28:10;
Mark 16:1–8; Luke 24:1–12; John 20:1–10

It was time.
Time for Jesus,
the Promised One,
to take away all our sins.

But as He prepared His heart and body
to be broken,
there was joy in His eyes.

Joy!

Jesus felt joy because He knew
that after His heartache
came healing.

Not just healing for Himself, but
healing for us all.
Because Jesus loves us . . . He felt joy.

You see, not everyone was happy Jesus was here.

Not everyone liked His
true teachings.
Not everyone liked His
amazing miracles.
Not everyone liked Jesus at all!

One dark night, some soldiers arrested Jesus.
They were mean to Him.
They hurt Him.
They told terrible lies about Him.

And then they did something very sad.
Very sad, and very bad.

They put Jesus on a cross . . .
and He died.

His followers were sad.
His disciples were sad.
His mother, Mary, was sad.
His friends and His family
and His believers were all so very sad.

Even a soldier who stood at the cross proclaimed,
"Truly this was the Son of God!"

And everyone cried.
They gently wrapped Jesus's body in cloths
and laid Him in a tomb.

But please, dear friend, don't feel hopeless.
Please, don't feel scared.
Please, please, keep reading,
because God did the most amazing,
the most wonderful,
the most awesome, outstanding,
gigantic miracle ever!

Are you ready for Good News?

After three days,

God raised Jesus from the dead!

He did! It's true!

Jesus's friends ran to the tomb and looked inside . . .
Gasp!

The tomb was empty.

Where did Jesus go?
they wondered.
Who took Him?

Beautiful, brilliant angels appeared and said,

**"Do not be afraid,
Jesus is not here!
He is risen!"**

Oh, yes! He is risen indeed.

Here is the Good News, my friend:
Jesus died for our sins,
but God raised Him from the dead.
Yes, Jesus was alive that day.
Jesus is still alive today.
And Jesus, our Savior, will be alive forevermore!

FAMILY TALK

Faith Foundation:

Jesus Takes Away Our Sin

Key Verse

He (Jesus) is the payment for our sins, and not only for our sins, but also for the sins of the whole world.

1 John 2:2

Sadly, Jesus was beaten and bruised and hung on a cross. But God, full of wisdom, had a plan. A good and wonderful plan. A plan He had known since the beginning of time.

You see, when Jesus was on the cross, He took the punishment for sin and died. But then, God the Father raised Jesus from the dead. Jesus rose in victory! And now, by faith in Jesus alone, no punishment for our sin is left for you and me. Jesus took it all—and in return we can have eternal life.

Adam and Eve looked forward to this day. Noah, Abraham, Joseph, and so many others believed that God would send the Promised One, a Savior who would take away our sin, so we can all live joyfully with God forever. And He did. God sent His son Jesus to be the Promised One, our Savior. Yes and Amen! God keeps His promises.

What is your favorite part of the Easter story?

What do you think the angel looked like?

FAMILY FUN

Cross and Butterfly

Option #1 Cut out a cross and decorate it any way you like. Hang these crosses on a door or window. Every time you see them, thank Jesus, the Promised One, for coming . . . for you.

Option #2 The butterfly is a symbol of the new life Jesus proclaimed at the resurrection and of the new life we have when we believe in Him. Make a beautiful butterfly using a coffee filter and food coloring. Let drops of food coloring fall on the coffee filter to create wonderful designs, or make spots and dots with colored markers. Then, gather the filter together in the middle and secure with a clothespin or a pipe cleaner. Hang your butterfly from the ceiling over your bed, and every time you see it, thank Jesus, the Promised One, for salvation.

Option #3 Draw a beautiful picture of the angels at the empty tomb.
Add this picture to your Bible Story Binder.

UP!

The Ascension—Acts 1:3–11

After Jesus rose from the dead,
He appeared to many people and
explained many things about the
kingdom of God.

Can you imagine how exciting it was
to see Jesus alive again?
Raised from the dead!

Jesus told His disciples to be ready,
because He promised . . .
**"I will send the Holy Spirit upon you
to fill you with power from heaven."**

But first, it was time for Jesus to go home
to His heavenly Father.

As the disciples watched in amazement,
Jesus ascended . . .

Up Up Up
into the sky,

Up Up Up
into the clouds,

Up Up Up
through the very gates
of heaven.

And now He sits
at the right hand of God.

From there, Jesus prays for us,
His people.
And He prepares a special place for us
so that we too
may someday happily
go home to heaven.

You see,
one day,
Jesus will return
in the full glory of God.

Look for the lightning to flash!
Listen for the trumpets to play!
Oh, yes,
Jesus will come back someday
so we can live joyfully with God forever.

What a great and glorious day!

FAMILY TALK

Faith Foundation:

Jesus Sits with God Forever

Key Verse

They were staring into the sky as He (Jesus) departed. Suddenly, two men in white clothes stood near them. They asked, "Why are you men from Galilee standing here looking at the sky? Jesus, who was taken from you to heaven, will come back in the same way that you saw him go to heaven."

Acts 1:10–11

Jesus was swept up to the clouds—up to heaven where He sits on His throne as King. There, Jesus prays for us and prepares a place for us to come and join Him. Yes, Jesus is coming back for us someday.

Isn't it good to know—Jesus is praying for you?
Isn't it wonderful to know—Jesus is preparing a place for you?
And isn't it amazing to know—Jesus is coming back for you?
Yes! Come, Lord Jesus!

Where did Jesus go when He ascended to the clouds?
What kind of place do you think Jesus is preparing for you?
What do you think it will be like when Jesus returns?

FAMILY FUN

"Pick-a-Prayer-to-Pray"

When we pray, our prayers go up, up, up directly to God. He hears every word we say and think . . . and He listens with love. So let's joyfully talk to the God of all.

Cut five cards out of stiff paper. On each card, write one of these fill-in-the-blank sentences. Decorate your cards and place them in a box or basket in your room. Each night draw out one or more cards and pray your very own prayers by filling in the blanks.

Praise: "Dear God, You are so great and I praise You for ____"

Confession: "Dear God, I am sorry for ____"

Thanks: "Dear God, I am so thankful for ____ and ____"

Supplication: "Dear God, please help me ____"

Intercession: "Dear God, please help my friend ____."

Jesus prayed to His heavenly Father often. You can talk to God anytime about anything from anywhere.

Draw a beautiful picture of Jesus ascending to His throne. Add this picture to your Bible Story Binder.

COME, HOLY SPIRIT

Pentecost—Acts 2:1–41

After Jesus went up to His Father in heaven,
His disciples gathered together in Jerusalem.

Suddenly, a wild rushing wind from heaven
filled the whole house.

WhoooOOOoooOOOOOOoosh!

And each disciple of Jesus was filled with the
Holy Spirit.

Little flickers of fire
like bright burning candle flames
rested gently on each person's head.

They stared at each other in amazement.
What's happening? they thought.

And then . . .
the disciples
opened their mouths
to speak.

But, guess what?

They did not understand the words that came out!

They did not speak in their own language.

No.

Instead, they spoke in many, many

different languages!

Curious crowds gathered.

Women from Rome.

Men from Judea.

Children from Egypt and Mesopotamia.

Traders from Libya, Asia, and more.

Merchants, leaders

the rich and the poor.

They all circled around the disciples

and heard about the

mighty works of God

each in their very own language.

How can this be?

The crowd wondered in amazement.

This must be a gift from God.

331

Peter
Jesus's friend and disciple
stood up and said,

"Jesus is the Promised One!
He died on the cross for you and me
and God raised Him from the dead.
Now He is exalted and seated with God,
and just as He promised
He has sent the Holy Spirit to us."

Deep down in their hearts,
the crowd knew this was true.

"Oh what,"
they cried out,
"Oh what should we do?"

"Be saved!"
Peter called out.

"Repent and be baptized
in the name of Jesus
for the forgiveness of your sins
and the Holy Spirit
will come and live
in your heart forever!"

And they did.

Man after man
woman after woman
stepped into the water, repented, and were
baptized.

Just that one day,
Three thousand people
proclaimed their faith in Jesus, the Promised One,
and received the Holy Spirit.

"The promise is for you and your children,"
Peter said, smiling.

And it still is.
Yes, the promise is for you and me!

FAMILY TALK

Faith Foundation:

Jesus Sends the Holy Spirit

> **Key Verse**
>
> I (Jesus) will ask the Father, and he will give you another helper who will be with you forever. That helper is the Spirit of Truth. . . . You know him, because he lives with you and will be in you.
>
> *John 14:16–17*

When you put your faith in Jesus as the Promised One, the Holy Spirit of God comes and lives within your heart forever. The Holy Spirit is active in the life of all believers of Jesus.

He gives us faith in Jesus, the Promised One.
He teaches and empowers us to do what is right.
He helps us to pray when we don't know what to say.
He gives us special gifts.
He comforts us when we are sad or lonely or confused.
And He loves us eternally!

What was your favorite part of this story?
What is the best part of having the Holy Spirit live in your heart?

FAMILY FUN

Still Small Voice

Option #1
Play a game of "Still Small Voice." Blindfold your child and go for a walk outdoors. The leader gently taps on the left or right shoulder to let the walker know which direction to turn. The Holy Spirit is like that; He is often a quiet voice we hear in our hearts telling us the right way to go.

Make a wind spiral.

Cut a 6- or 9-inch circle out of a foam sheet. Starting at the outside, cut around and around—about ½ inch wide—making a spiral all the way to the center of the circle. Now, hold up the spiral and blow on it. Does it move? Tape the inside of the spiral to a straw. Hold it in front of a fan. Can you see the wind? No. But it is real. So it is with God's Holy Spirit. You can't see Him, but you can see what He does.

Option #2
Draw a picture of this exciting day. Add this picture to your Bible Story Binder.

PAUL'S GREAT ADVENTURE

Acts 9:1–31

There was a man named
Paul.
He hated followers of Jesus.
So Paul tried to stop them
from believing in God's Son.

He walked
to town after town after town.
And talked
to crowd after crowd after crowd
fighting against God's people.

But God
had a different plan
for Paul.

One day, as Paul was riding on the road
to the town of Damascus . . .

Flash!

a bright light blinded Paul,
making him fall to the ground.

Oomph!

A strong loud voice asked,
"Paul, why are you against Me?"

"Who . . . who . . . who are you, Lord?"
asked Paul as he shivered and shook.
"I am Jesus."

Paul knew he had been wrong.
At that very minute,
Paul turned his heart toward God's Son.
"Jesus, you are the Savior!"
Paul put all his faith in Jesus that day.
He was filled with the Holy Spirit and was baptized.

Paul began a lifetime of adventure,
as he walked
to town after town after town.
And talked
to crowd after crowd after crowd,
telling them this good news:

"We are saved by grace
through faith
in Jesus."

Oh, yes!
Paul's great adventure took him far and wide
over tall mountains and across wild seas
to city
after city
after city
after city
to tell all the world:

"Jesus
the Promised One
died for our sins
and rose again in victory
so that you
and I
and everyone who believes
can be forgiven
and live in the
everlasting joy
of knowing God
for eternity."

FAMILY TALK

Faith Foundation:

Jesus Wants Everyone to Know the Good News

Key Verse

I'm not ashamed of the Good News. It is God's power to save everyone who believes.

Romans 1:16

Oh, yes! Paul told everyone he met about Jesus, because Jesus wants everyone to know the Good News. Paul told them, "Jesus is God's only Son. Put your faith in Jesus . . . the Promised One."

He told tall people and short people. He told rich people and poor people. He told young people and old people. He told people here—people there—people everywhere about the Good News of Jesus.

Did you know God wants *you* to tell other people about Jesus too? It's true. Telling others about Jesus is a great adventure!

Can you tell other people about Jesus like Paul did?
Who can you tell? What will you tell them?
You can tell people about Jesus anytime and anywhere.

FAMILY FUN

The Good News Newspaper

 Option #1 Make a Good News newspaper. Paul is still telling people about Jesus—through his letters in the Bible. Just like Paul you can write the truth about Jesus, the Promised One, and proclaim to others the way to be forgiven forever. Have every person in the family write an article or draw a picture about Jesus. Here are some ideas:

Describe heaven. How do we get there?

What is something amazing that Jesus did?

Why have you decided to follow Jesus?

Write a prayer of praise.

Write your own letter to God.

Draw a picture of you and Jesus together.

Make a simple crossword puzzle.

Pass out copies of your Good News newspaper to others. How many other ways can you think of to spread the Good News of Jesus Christ? Now, go out and do them.

Option #2 Draw a picture of the Bible which Paul helped to write. Add this picture to your Bible Story Binder.

ALL THINGS NEW

Heaven—Revelation 21–22

Jesus said,

"I make all things new!"

and He does.

He loves us and makes us a new heart to love God.
He adopts us and makes us
a new family as children of God.
He forgives us and makes us a new life,
free and happy with God.

But that is not all . . .
Oh, no! There is more!

Jesus makes one more thing new for us:
eternity.

An eternal life, forever,
in heaven
with God.

What do you think heaven is like?
The Bible describes heaven like this . . .

It's like a city . . .
a giant city . . .
a giant glowing city of God.

It's made of pure gold and
sparkles like a jewel.

There are
sapphires
emeralds
topaz
and amethyst.

Yes, every kind of precious stone
adds to the glory of this holy place.

There are twelve gates
surrounding this sparkling city,
each made of an enormous single pearl.
And these pearly gates are never closed or locked.
Everyone is forever safe in the city of God.

In heaven there is no sun.
There is no moon.

That is because the

glory of God

lights up the city with a warm
cozy
brilliant
light.

God's goodness
His mercy
His holiness and power and love
shine out from Him
and illuminate all of heaven.

What a wonderful light that must be!

A river of the water of life

clear, like crystal,
flows from the center of the great city.

Beside the river
a special tree grows.

It is the tree of life.

It bears twelve different kinds of fruit.

A new one each month.

Amazing!

And the Bible says there is healing in its leaves.

In the center of the city, God sits on a crystal throne,

A glorious rainbow of colors
circle around the throne
and flashes of lightning
shoot out from Him.

Angels shout out to one another:
"Holy Holy Holy
is the Lord God Almighty!
Who was and is and is to come!"

Joining in with loud voices are the multitudes of
happy people
like mighty rushing waters
and great claps of thunder
singing in praise,

**"Hallelujah!
For the Lord God Almighty reigns!"**

But best of all,
the Bible says we will see our God and Savior

face-to-face

**and He will wipe
every tear
from our eyes.**

No more pain.
No more death.
No more sorrow or sadness ever.

Only joy!
Only love!
Only peace and praise and perfection.

Yes, the best thing about heaven is

God Himself!

And we,
the family of God,
will live joyfully with God forever
and ever
and ever
and ever
and ever
and ever
and ever!

Praise God!
Hallelujah!

FAMILY TALK

Faith Foundation:

Our Future Hope and Promise

 Key Verse

I heard a loud voice from the throne say, "God lives with humans! God will make his home with them, and they will be his people. God himself will be with them and be their God. He will wipe every tear from their eyes."

Revelation 21:3–4

What is the best part of heaven?
The city of jewels?
The glowing glory of God as its light?
The crystal clear river of life?
The fabulous fruit from the tree of life?
The colors and praises surrounding God's throne?
No.
The best part of heaven is being with God face-to-face in His gentle, warm, loving embrace. Heaven is heavenly because of God Himself!

What is your favorite description of heaven?
Why do you want to go there someday?
Have you trusted Jesus, the Promised One, to save you?

FAMILY FUN

Heavenly Mural

Option #1 Make a huge mural of heaven on a large piece of butcher or poster paper. Divide the poster into sections, one space for each person. Each family member can draw what they think is most special about heaven. You can draw:

> the tree of life
> sparkling jewels
> streets of gold
> angels
> glowing light of God
> people rejoicing
> Jesus on His throne
> river of life

Draw anything from the story, or read Revelation 21–22 to get other ideas.

 Option #2 Draw a beautiful picture of heaven. Add this picture to your Bible Book Binder.

THE GOSPEL EXPLAINED

Romans

Yes, my friend, God's promise is for you.
Did you like the stories? Do you want to hear more?
Listen to these verses from the Bible
that explain God's awesome promise:

**"Because all people have sinned,
they have fallen short of God's glory."**
Romans 3:23

Remember Adam and Eve?
Well, just like them, all of us have sinned.
We often choose to turn away from God and disobey Him.

This sin in our hearts separates us from God
and keeps us from living joyfully with Him.
And our sin must be punished.

But God,
in His mercy and great love,
wanted to make a way for us to be saved
from our sin.
So . . . He sent the one and only way.
God sent His Son,

Jesus, the Promised One.

What did Jesus, the Promised One, do?
**"Christ died for us while we were still sinners.
This demonstrates God's love for us."**
Romans 5:8

Oh, yes!
God showed His great and awesome
deep and wide
abundant and amazing
love for us
at the cross.

When Jesus died,
He took all the punishment for our sin.
Jesus took it all!
Now, we can stand forgiven and free.

And now, God can pour out on us:
His love
His forgiveness
His mercy
His blessing
His kindness
His gentleness
His compassion
and so much more!

But, how do we receive this free gift of forgiveness
and eternal life with God?

**"If you declare that Jesus is Lord, and believe that
God brought him back to life, you will be saved."**
Romans 10:9

We are saved by faith in Jesus.
So . . . proclaim your faith!
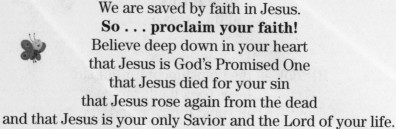
Believe deep down in your heart
that Jesus is God's Promised One
that Jesus died for your sin
that Jesus rose again from the dead
and that Jesus is your only Savior and the Lord of your life.

**"Whoever calls on the name of the Lord
will be saved."**
Romans 10:13

**"Now that we have God's approval by faith,
we have peace with God
because of what our Lord Jesus Christ has done."**
Romans 5:1

Yes,
for those who put their faith in Jesus,
there is peace with God.
No fear of punishment.
No!
No separation from God.
No!

**Only a loving relationship with the God of All.
Oh, yes!**

Now we may live joyfully with God
today
tomorrow
and forever.

And just listen to this promise:

**"I am convinced that nothing can ever separate us
from God's love which Christ Jesus our Lord shows us."**
Romans 8:38

Nothing will ever take away God's love for us.

We stand secure and solid in God's love.

He loves us eternally—He cannot love us more.
He loves us forever—He will not love us less.
Nothing we do will ever, ever change His love for us in
Jesus.

And someday, because of Jesus,
we will go to heaven and live joyfully with God forever.

What Good News!

**"Listen, now is God's acceptable time!
Now is the day of salvation!"**
2 Corinthians 6:2

Would you like to declare your faith in Jesus today?
You can.
Today or any day.

If your heart is longing for Jesus, please pray with me.

Dear God,
    Thank you for giving me faith in your Son, Jesus, the Promised One. I'm sorry that I have sinned. But I believe that Jesus, my Lord and Savior, took all my punishment on the cross for me and by faith I am forgiven and free.
    Because Jesus rose again to life, someday I will go to live with You, God, in heaven forever. Thank You for Your Holy Spirit, who comes into my life. Yes, thank You, God for saving me by Your grace.
    In Jesus's name, Amen.

AND SO . . .

God's wise plan of salvation

has been the same from the beginning of time.

Salvation by faith through grace alone . . .

in Jesus, God's Promised One.

Let's remember all the stories together!

Why did Jesus come?

He came as God's image—like He made Adam and Eve.

He came as the Promised One—

like God promised in the garden.

He came to be the one way of salvation—

like the ark that saved Noah.

He came to be our father—like father Abraham.

He came to fulfill God's plan—like God did through Joseph.

He came to free His people—like God did through Moses.

He came to live a perfect life—like God had spoken in the
Ten Commandments.

He came as our king, to defeat the enemy—
like God did through David.

He came to be at work for us—like God did for Esther.

He came to be the wisdom of God—
like the wise sayings of Proverbs.

He came to proclaim the praise of God—
like the writers of Psalms.

He came to bring hope—
like God proclaimed through the prophets.

Jesus came to be the Lamb of God—
like John announced at His baptism.
He came to make us see—
like He opened the eyes of Bartimaeus.
He came to bring new life—
like He raised Lazarus from the dead.
He came to show His power—
like He calmed the stormy sea.
He came to be our foundation—
like the house built on the rock.
He came to find us and make us His own—
like the parable of the lost lamb.
He came to make us children of God—
like the little children He loved.

He came to be our king—

like He came at the triumphant entry.

He came to take away our sin—like He did on the cross.

He came to bring us new life—like His resurrection to life.

He came to return to God—like His ascension.

He came to give us the Holy Spirit—

like He sent on the day of Pentecost.

And Jesus came to be

the one and only way to heaven.

He came to take away our sin

and give us forgiveness.

He came to give us faith

so we can live joyfully with God forever!

And so, my friend,
this is not the end.
This is only the beginning of

Your life of faith in Jesus . . .

the Promised One!

Amen.

Acknowledgments

We would like to thank the dedicated and talented Revell team for the incredible job they did in taking *My Favorite Bible* from manuscript to finished book:

Andrea Doering, acquisitions editor

Mary Wenger, editor

Paula Gibson, art director

Mike Williams, designer

Twila Bennett, senior director of marketing

Janelle Mahlmann, assistant marketing manager

We'd also like to thank Ariel Pang for her delightful illustrations. Her creative gifts have brought our words to life beyond anything we could have imagined!

A special thank you to Lee Hough, our literary agent at Alive Communications.

Thank you also to MOPS (Mothers of Preschoolers) for their encouragement and endorsement.

May the countless hours spent on this book by each member of this great, godly team touch the hearts and lives of children everywhere—bringing one child at a time one step closer to faith in the gospel of Jesus Christ.

Rondi DeBoer sold her first series at age fifteen and now has more than 430,000 copies of her books in print. After graduating from Washington State University in elementary education and studying at Multnomah Biblical Seminary, she went on to become a classical Christian teacher. Now she spends her time homeschooling her three daughters and eagerly awaits the arrival of a fourth daughter from China. She and her husband, Brian, live in Washington with their family.

Christine Tangvald has been writing for children for more than twenty-five years, with nearly one hundred titles to her name and almost 3.5 million books in print. After earning her elementary education degree, she worked with children for more than twenty years. Her passion is to personalize God and make Him real and alive to small children. She lives in Washington with her husband, Roald.

Ariel Pang is an award-winning illustrator whose vibrant, colorful work has graced the pages of several children's books. She makes her home in Taiwan.

Want to be the best mom possible? You are not alone.

At MOPS you can enjoy real friendships, personal growth, and spiritual hope as part of a mothering community.

Get connected today!

Mothers of Preschoolers

2370 S. Trenton Way, Denver CO 80231 ■ 888.910.MOPS

For information on MOPS International visit **MOPS.org**

Better Moms Make A Better World

GOD'S WORD for Girls
Two-Tone Duravella

GOD'S WORD for Girls
Pink Hardcover

**GOD'S WORD for Girls
Raspberry Swirl Duravella**
$29.99 • 978-0-8010-1365-2

**GOD'S WORD for Girls
Purple/Pink Duravella**
$29.99 • 978-0-8010-7257-4

**GOD'S WORD for Girls
Pink Hardcover**
$27.99 • 978-0-8010-1326-3

Girls, now you can have your very own Bible with tons of great features made just for you:

- ◎ *Book Intros*—tell you the big ideas in the book you're about to read
- ◎ *Devotions*—help you read, think, and pray
- ◎ *Genuine Heroines*—show you women of the Bible you'll want to be like
- ◎ *Women's World*—uncover fascinating facts about what life was like for a woman in Bible times
- ◎ *Be All You Can Be*—show you how to think and act the way God wants
- ◎ *Drawings, Illustrations, and Maps*—bring the Bible to life

GOD'S WORD for Girls has all this, plus the full text of the Bible in the accurate and readable *GOD'S WORD* Translation, so you can become the woman God wants you to be.

BakerBooks
a division of Baker Publishing Group
www.BakerBooks.com

**GOD'S WORD.
TRANSLATION**

www.godswordtranslation.org

GOD'S WORD for Boys
Two-Tone Duravella

GOD'S WORD for Boys
Blue Hardcover

GOD'S WORD for Boys
Hunter Green/Khaki Duravella
$29.99 • 978-0-8010-1364-5

GOD'S WORD for Boys
Blue/Light Blue Duravella
$29.99 • 978-0-8010-7255-0

GOD'S WORD for Boys
Blue Hardcover
$27.99 • 978-0-8010-1325-6

Boys, now you can have your very own Bible with tons of great features made just for you:

- ⊚ Book Intros—tell you the big ideas in the book you're about to read
- ⊚ Devotions—help you read, think, and pray
- ⊚ Genuine Heroes—show you men of the Bible you'll want to be like
- ⊚ Men's World—uncover fascinating facts about what life was like for a man in Bible times
- ⊚ Be All You Can Be—show you how to think and act the way God wants
- ⊚ Drawings, Illustrations, and Maps—bring the Bible to life

GOD'S WORD for Boys has all this, plus the full text of the Bible in the accurate and readable GOD'S WORD Translation, so you can become the man God wants you to be.

BakerBooks
a division of Baker Publishing Group
www.BakerBooks.com

GOD'S WORD TRANSLATION

www.godswordtranslation.org

KJV Study Bible for Boys

**KJV Study Bible for Boys
Blue Hardcover**
$24.99 • 978-0-8010-7266-6

**KJV Study Bible for Boys
Blue Duravella**
$29.99 • 978-0-8010-7267-3

**KJV Study Bible for Boys
Blue Prism Duravella**
$29.99 • 978-0-8010-7265-9

KJV Study Bible for Girls

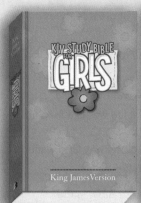

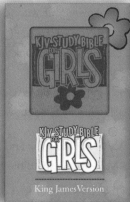

**KJV Study Bible for Girls
Pink Hardcover**
$24.99 • 978-0-8010-7269-7

**KJV Study Bible for Girls
Pink Duravella**
$29.99 • 978-0-8010-7268-0

**KJV Study Bible for Girls
Pink Prism Duravella**
$29.99 • 978-0-8010-7270-3

 BakerBooks
a division of Baker Publishing Group
www.BakerBooks.com